Super Bizarre

LIKE INSANE!

BIZARRE
SUPERSTITIONS

BY CHRISTOPHER COOPER

Hello this
is my book!
PUT IT DOWN!! JK :D

Be patient with a bad neighbor: He may move or have some bad luck.

Everything has an end—except a sausage, which has two.

Never bolt your door with a boiled carrot.

A woman should serve her husband roasted owl if she wants him to be obedient to her every wish.

Drinking water in which a mouse had been boiled was a remedy for inflammation of the tonsils.

You can protect your home from ghosts by removing a door and hanging it with the hinges on the other side.

Break the shell of a boiled egg after eating it: that will prevent witches from using it to travel in.

It is good luck to encounter nuns—but not if they are walking away from you.

BIZARRE SUPERSTITIONS

BY CHRISTOPHER COOPER

The World's Wackiest Proverbs, Rituals, and Beliefs

Property of :

STERLING

New York / London
www.sterlingpublishing.com

STERLING and the distinctive Sterling logo are registered
trademarks of Sterling Publishing Co., Inc.

10 9 8 7 6 5 4 3 2 1

Published by Sterling Publishing Co., Inc.
387 Park Avenue South, New York, NY 10016
© 2009 Anova Book Company Limited
Distributed in Canada by Sterling Publishing
c/o Canadian Manda Group, 165 Dufferin Street
Toronto, Ontario, Canada M6K 3H6
Distributed in the United Kingdom by GMC
Distribution Services
Castle Place, 166 High Street, Lewes, East Sussex,
England BN7 1XU
Distributed in Australia by Capricorn Link
(Australia) Pty. Ltd.
P.O. Box 704, Windsor, NSW 2756, Australia

Printed by NPE Print Communications Pte Ltd, Singapore

Sterling ISBN 978-1-4027-6831-6

For information about custom editions, special sales,
premium and corporate purchases, please contact
Sterling Special Sales
Department at 800-805-5489 or
specialsales@sterlingpublishing.com.

CONTENTS:

PROVERBS

SCANDINAVIA

NORWAY

There is no shame in clothing you have not cut yourself.

The headless army can be in for a hard time.

It's bad to get ashamed over a thing well grasped.

Who marries in too great haste ends up as a half-slave at his place.

On the road between the homes of friends, grass does not grow.

Poor thanks is the way of the world.

It's no shame to look into the warm spring sun and regret a lost limb.

Heroism consists of hanging on one minute longer.

It is better to feed one cat than many mice.

The lame man runs if he has to.

FINLAND

Life is uncertain so eat your **dessert** first.

Love came in a paper bag, said the maiden when she got a letter from her sweetheart.

On the gallows, the first night is the worst.

War does not determine who is right, only who is remaining.

A man comes back from beyond the seas, not from under the sod.

Work doesn't scare him, but he could lie down near it and sleep.

Time for the mouse to yawn when it's half inside the cat.

Don't mistake the bone for meat, nor a sheep's head for a roasted turnip.

Don't go to the sauna if you're not itching.

The box chooses its lid.

The frost drives the pig home.

Laughter from long joy, a fart from laughing long.

Even the crow sings with its own voice.

Poverty is no joy, although it sometimes makes you laugh.

He stares like a cow at a new gate.

The forest will answer you in the way you call to it.

If tar, hard liquor, and the sauna do not cure, the disease is fatal.

SWEDEN

A piece of bread in the pocket is worth more than a feather in the hat.

Don't throw away the old bucket until you're sure the new one holds water.

If a blind man leads another, they both fall down together.

Don't sell the fur until the bear has been shot.

Don't let your sorrow come higher than your knees.

Fear less, hope more, eat less, chew more, whine less, breathe more, talk less, say more, hate less, love more, and all good things will be yours.

Advice should be viewed from behind.

The best place to find a helping hand is at the end of your own arm.

"Sour" said the fox about rowanberries.

DENMARK

After three days, both fish and guests begin to smell.

A head is not to be cut off because it is scabby.

What you cannot say briefly you do not know.

God gives every bird its food but does not drop it into the nest.

A little dog, a cow without horns, and a short man, are generally proud.

Judge a maiden at the kneading trough, not at the dance.

A woman may be ever so old, but if you set her on fire, she will jump.

Children and drunken men speak the truth.

For a good dinner and a gentle wife, you can afford to wait.

Every little fish expects to become a whale.

Better a salt herring on your own table, than a fresh pike on another man's.

Give to a pig when it grunts, and a child when it cries, and you will have a fine pig, and a bad child.

He who can sit upon a stone and feed himself should not move.

Everything has an end—except a sausage, which has two.

A man who sows peas on the highway does not get all the pods into his barn.

Many a cow stands in the meadow and looks wistfully at the common.

He who herds with wolves learns to howl.

Help is good everywhere, except in the porridge bowl.

It is a bold mouse that makes her nest in the cat's ear.

He who has a white horse and a fair wife is seldom without trouble.

He who has no falcon, must hunt with owls.

The best manure is under the farmer's shoe.

Praise the child, and you make love to the mother.

Sparrows should not dance with cranes; their legs are too short.

The dog's kennel is not the place to keep a sausage.

You must walk a long while behind a wild goose before you find an ostrich feather.

You cannot drink and whistle at the same time.

When neighbors quarrel, lookers-on are more apt to add fuel than water.

EASTERN EUROPE

RUSSIA

There will be trouble if the cobbler starts making pies.

Peace lasts till the army comes, and the army lasts till peace comes.

You cannot break through a wall with your forehead.

A word of kindness is better than a fat pie.

Tell God the truth, but give the judge money.

A good merchant has neither money nor goods.

A cat always knows whose meat it eats.

Until you have smoked out the bees, you can't eat the honey.

Even a blind pig finds an acorn every once in a while.

Fear the goat from the front, the horse from the rear, and man from all sides.

The tallest blade of grass is the first to be cut by the scythe.

Having a good wife and rich cabbage soup, seek not other things.

You do not really understand something unless you can explain it to your grandmother.

God wanted to chastise mankind, so he sent lawyers.

Every vegetable has its time.

The wolf will hire himself out very cheaply as a shepherd.

If you put your nose into water, you will also wet your cheeks.

Sit a beggar at your table and he will soon put his feet on it.

Bad luck is fertile.

The coat is quite new; only the holes are old.

It is easier for the horse when a woman is off the cart.

If you feel the need to work, take a nap; the need will pass.

HUNGARY

A prudent man does not make the goat his gardener.

He who cannot speak Arabic should not speak Arabic.

Whoever gets mixed up with bran will be eaten by pigs.

The owl tells the sparrow that her head is big.

Former highwaymen make the best policemen.

Believe in women as in the weather in April.

A fool stumbles twice at the same stone.

Tell me who your friend is, and I'll tell you who you are.

Having no ointment and box, why do you pose as hairdresser?

Many homes burn inside but it is not seen outside.

Two dogs never agree on one bone.

A kiss without a beard is like an egg without salt.

A red-haired dog, a red-haired horse, a red-haired man—none of them are good.

Even an old goat likes to lick salt.

He can live even on flat ice.

Long sausages and short sermons are good.

He that is not a master of something is a butcher of it.

He who is sitting in the reeds makes a whistle of his choice.

Do not stir the manure if you do not want the smell to get even worse.

He will disappear like a gray donkey in the fog.

An ox remains an ox even if driven to Vienna.

He knows as much about it as a hen does about the alphabet.

Sing the song of the man whose cart you sit on.

An arrow once shot is hard to get back.

Better a sparrow in the hand than a pigeon on the roof.

The discontented child cries for toasted snow.

It is better to have your house burn down twice rather than move once.

He who is (too) curious shall grow old soon.

He who cannot cut the bread evenly cannot get on well with people.

Czech beer makes beautiful bodies.

A hundred bakers, a hundred millers, and a hundred tailors are three hundred thieves.

WESTERN EUROPE

GERMANY

A swindler who cannot pass off mouse-turd for pepper has not learned his trade.

All skill is in vain when an angel pees in the touch-hole of your musket.

Affectation is a greater injury to the face than smallpox.

Bargains are costly.

Coffee and love are best when they are hot.

A lawyer and the wheel of the cart must be greased.

A pack of cards is the devil's prayer book.

FRANCE

The hunchback does not see his hump, but sees that of his fellow man.

It is better to lose a witty remark than a friend.

Insane and simple is the ewe that makes the wolf his confessor.

Corn grows well in a small field.

A muzzled cat never took mice.

A crooked log makes a good fire.

Eagles don't breed doves.

A woman's advice is no great thing, but he who won't take it is a fool.

A glaring sunny morning, a woman that talks Latin, and a child reared on wine never come to a good end.

A fence between makes love more keen.

A fine girl and a tattered gown always find something to hook them.

A big nose never spoiled a handsome face.

A clown enriched knows neither relation nor friend.

A crooked stick will have a crooked shadow.

A fool's heart dances on his lips.

A deaf husband and a blind wife are always a happy couple.

A man with a watch knows what time it is. A man with two watches is never sure.

A woman and a melon are hard to choose.

A person is unlucky who falls on his back and breaks his nose.

A woman and a ship ever want mending.

A woman's tongue is her sword, and she does not let it rust.

He is a very bad manager of honey who leaves nothing to lick off his fingers.

Better be an old man's darling than a young man's slave.

He is like a singed cat, better than he looks.

The fox says of the mulberries, when he cannot get at them, they are not good at all.

He who would go to sea for pleasure would go to hell for a pastime.

He who sees leather cut asks for a thong.

One may steal nothing except a lawyer's purse.

It is a stupid goose that listens to the fox preach.

It is a sorry house in which the cock is silent and the hen crows.

It is good to beat a proud man when he is alone.

A man should choose a wife with his ears, rather than with his eyes.

War is much too serious a matter to be left in the hands of the military.

When all you have is a hammer, everything looks like a nail.

The miser and the pig are of no use till they are both dead.

Think much, say little, write less.

To grow rich one has only to turn his back on God.

Where the hostess is pretty, the wine is good.

To a good cat, a good rat.

Write injuries in the sand and kindnesses in marble.

IRELAND

Marriages are all happy. It's having breakfast together that causes all the trouble.

Drink is the curse of the land. It makes you fight with your neighbor. It makes you **shoot** at your landlord and it makes you **miss him.**

Firelight will not let you read fine stories but it's warm and you won't see the dust on the floor.

It's better to return from the center of the ford than drown in the flood.

Put a beggar on horseback and he'll ride to hell.

Men are like bagpipes; no sound comes from them until they're full.

It is no time to go for the doctor when the patient is dead.

What butter and whiskey will not cure, there's no cure for.

There's little value in the single cow.

Going in is not the same as going out.

The drunkard takes the roof from his own house and puts it on the publican's house.

The lake is no heavier for the duck which is on it.

I'll go there tonight for evening is speedier than morning.

Hunger is a good sauce.

He may die of wind but he'll never die of wisdom.

Nature breaks out through the eyes of the cat.

The poor lack much, but the greedy more.

Never bolt your door with a boiled carrot.

The old pipe gives the sweetest smoke.

A boy's best friend is his mother, and there's no tie stronger than her apron string.

It's no use boiling your cabbage twice.

If it's drowning you're after, don't torment yourself with shallow water.

A man takes a drink, the drink takes a drink, the drink takes a drink, the drink takes the man.

The pig in the sty doesn't know the pig going along the road.

It's no use carrying an umbrella if your shoes are leaking.

The one who opens his mouth the most, 'tis he who opens his purse the least.

ENGLAND

Scratch an Englishman, and you'll find a seaman.

He who takes the devil into his boat must carry him over the sound.

When it begins to thump its rib with its tail, look out for thunder, lightning, and hail.

When a cow tries to scratch its ear, it means a shower be very near.

Servants, like ornaments, should be kept in their proper places.

Spring has come when you can put your foot on three daisies.

In a cat's eye, all things belong to cats.

Every mile in winter is two.

A lie well stuck to is as good as the truth.

SCOTLAND

The devil's boots don't creak.

Pride that dines wi'
vanity sups wi'
contempt.

**Give a man
luck and fling
him in the sea.**

A deaf man will
hear the clink o'
money.

**Willful waste
makes woeful want.**

As the fool thinks, the bell clinks.

SPAIN

Raise a raven,
and it will peck
out your eyes.

For lack of good
men, they made
my father
mayor.

To a skinny dog, all are fleas.

**When the Indian slides on his
backside, there's no way to stop him.**

If your wife wants to throw you off the roof, try to find a low one.

Halfway is twelve miles when you have fourteen miles to go.

God gives almonds to those who have no teeth.

It's better to arrive at the right moment than to be invited.

Never advise anyone to go to war or to marry.

Better a quiet death than a public misfortune

Blessed is he who expects nothing, for he shall never be disappointed.

Books are hindrances to persisting stupidity.

He who has a good harvest must put up with a few thistles.

It is better to conceal one's knowledge than to reveal one's ignorance.

If you want good service, serve yourself.

He who marries a widow will often have a dead man's head thrown into the dish.

Love is like war; begin when you like and leave off when you can.

Let your heart guide your head in evil matters.

Visit your aunt, but not every day of the year.

The best mirror is an old friend.

ITALY

He who has money to throw away, let him employ workmen, and not stand by.

A new broom is good for three days.

Below the navel there is neither religion nor truth.

A drowning man would clutch at razors.

Curses are like processions; they return to where they set out.

Does your neighbor love you? Lend him a sequin.

Eggs have no business dancing with stones.

He who is an ass and thinks himself a stag finds his mistake when he comes to leap the ditch.

Even a frog would bite if it had teeth.

Never let the sun go down on your anger.

Every dog is allowed one bite.

Every time history repeats itself the price goes up.

No sooner is the law made than its evasion is discovered.

He who wants milk should not sit in the middle of a field and wait for a cow to back up to him.

PACIFIC ISLANDS

MAORI

The brave man who climbs trees is food for their roots.

Persist in all things as resolutely as you persist in eating.

AFRICA

A bird does not change its feathers because the weather is bad.

A man who is trampled to death by an elephant must have been blind and deaf.

A sick person cannot survive if a greedy eater is allowed nearby.

A masked performer who tries too hard to outclass his colleagues may expose his backside.

Do not call to a dog with a whip in your hand.

An oil lamp feels proud to give light, even though it uses itself up.

He who is afraid of doing too much always does too little.

Do not tell the man who is carrying you that he stinks.

Indecision is like a stepchild: If he does not wash his hands, he is called dirty; if he does, he is told he is wasting water.

He who is being carried does not realize how far the town is.

It is not only the hyena—even the snail arrives at its destination.

It is the toothless animal that arrives first at the base of the fruit tree, to eat its fill before others arrive.

It is when there is a stampede that the person with big buttocks becomes conscious of his load.

No one tests the depth of the river with both feet.

One camel does not make fun of another camel's hump.

The end of an ox is beef, and the end of a lie is grief.

The fly that has no one to advise it follows the corpse into the grave.

The goat that cries the loudest is not the one that will eat the most.

The leech that does not let go, even when it is filled, dies on the dry land.

When a ripe fruit sees an honest man, it drops.

When a man's coat is threadbare, it is easy to pick a hole in it.

When the master is absent, the frogs hop into the house.

When a woman prepares a dish which others dislike, she claims that she prepared it to suit her own taste.

When the bee comes to your house, let her have beer; you may wish to visit her house some day.

When spiders unite, they can tie down a lion.

Whether the knife falls on the melon or the melon on the knife, it is the melon that suffers.

MOROCCO

An old cat will not learn how to dance.

Either do as your neighbors do, or move away.

If you are a peg, endure the knocking; if you are a mallet, strike.

MADAGASCAR

A canoe does not know who is king. When it turns over, everyone gets wet.

A patient who can swallow food makes the nurse doubtful.

An egg does not fight a rock.

Do not treat your loved one like the swinging door that you are fond of but push back and forth.

The lazy man who goes to borrow a spade says, "I hope I will not find one."

Do not be like a miser who saves for those who will bury him.

Cross in a crowd and the crocodile won't eat you.

Like roosters' tail feathers: pretty but always behind.

Disgraced—like a man whose own pet bites him.

SOUTHEAST AFRICA

Help comes in two ways: death or healing.

There is no season of heavy rains without mosquitoes.

The fear of God is not wearing a white turban.

When you play with a lion, do not put your hand in its mouth.

You may climb a thorn tree, and be unable to come down again.

When a fool becomes enlightened, the wise man is in trouble.

If you can't manage horses, what will you feed the elephants?

A man who waters his neighbor's cattle must first put his foot in the waterhole.

IRAQ

A man profits more by the sight of an idiot than by the orations of the learned.

A wise man associating with vice-ridden ones becomes an idiot; a dog traveling with good men grows wise.

An army of sheep led by a lion would defeat an army of lions led by a sheep.

All mankind is divided into three classes: those that are immoveable, those that are moveable, and those that move.

If you have to be a beggar, make sure you knock only at the largest gates.

If you buy cheap meat, when it boils you will smell what you have saved.

If the camel once gets his nose in the tent, the rest of him will follow.

If you stop every time a dog barks, your road will never end.

AFGHANISTAN

Don't show me the palm tree; show me the dates.

Only stretch your foot to the length of your blanket.

Five fingers are brothers but not equals.

If you deal in camels, make the doors high.

When the tiger kills, the jackal profits.

AZERBAIJAN

Saying "honey, honey" won't make your mouth sweet.

Until the lions have their historians, tales of the hunt will always glorify the hunter.

EGYPT

Be patient with a bad neighbor: He may move or have some bad luck.

Bed is the poor man's opera.

Put a rope around your neck and many will be happy to drag you along.

KURDISTAN

If watching could make you skillful, every dog would become a butcher.

It is easier to make a camel jump a ditch than to make a fool listen to reason.

Many will show you the way once your cart has overturned.

A cup of coffee may commit one to forty years of friendship.

Of everything else the newest; but of friends, the oldest.

The devil tempts all, but the idle man tempts the devil.

It is easy to catch a serpent with someone else's hand.

PALESTINE

Every sheep is hung by its own leg.

The eye cannot rise above the eyebrow.

PERSIA

A drowning man is not troubled by rain.

A stone thrown at the right time is better than gold given at the wrong time.

SYRIA

Good things often come to those who cannot benefit from them.

The camel limped and blamed its split lip.

He married the monkey for its money; the money went and the monkey stayed a monkey.

Trusting people is like trusting water to remain in a sieve.

The cock that will be eloquent crows while still in the egg.

When I decided to sell coffins, people decided not to die.

TURKESTAN

You may hide the disease, but you won't be able to hide the death.

Even if the world is flooded, the duck feels safe.

You can't take back your spit.

TURKEY

A threadbare coat is armor proof against highwaymen.

Call your husband cuckold in jest and he'll never suspect you.

Having two ears and one tongue, we should listen twice as much as we speak.

Call the bear "Uncle" till you are safe across the bridge.

If you speak the truth, better keep a foot in the stirrup.

Man is harder than iron, stronger than stone, and more fragile than a rose.

Two captains will sink the ship.

Two watermelons cannot be held under one arm.

SoUTHWEST ASIA

INDIA

Do not blame God for having created the tiger, but thank him for not having given it wings.

Pray one hour before going to war, two hours before going to sea, and three hours before getting married.

I have lanced many boils, but none pained like my own.

The sieve says to the needle, "You have a hole in your head."

Saints fly only in the eyes of their disciples.

Those who hunt deer sometimes find tigers.

To lend is to buy a quarrel.

When an elephant is in trouble even a frog will kick him.

Keep five yards from a carriage, ten yards from a horse, and a hundred yards from an elephant. But the distance one should keep from a wicked man cannot be measured.

The reputation lost for a betel nut cannot be regained by donating an elephant.

Seeing the peacock, the rooster spread his wings.

Living in water and being an enemy of the crocodile is not good.

If you need a job to be done, be prepared to fall at the feet of a donkey.

KASHMIR

One man's beard is on fire, and another man warms his hands on it.

One man can burn water, whereas another cannot even burn oil.

I bought the nettle, sowed the nettle, and then the nettle stung me.

One and one are sometimes eleven.

CHINA

Like waiting for a rabbit to bump its head upon a tree in order to catch it.

Man's heart is a snake that would swallow an elephant: it is never satisfied.

Flowing water never goes bad; door hinges never gather termites.

Sparrows who emulate peacocks are likely to break a thigh.

A bird does not sing because it has an answer. It sings because it has a song.

You won't help shoots grow by pulling them.

The wise forget insults, as the ungrateful a kindness.

People dream different dreams while on the same bed.

A person who says it cannot be done should not interrupt the man doing it.

Weasels often come and say "Happy New Year" to the chickens.

A single untried popular remedy often throws the scientific doctor into hysterics.

Do not use a hatchet to remove a fly from your friend's forehead.

An ignorant doctor is no better than a murderer.

A crisis is an opportunity riding the dangerous wind.

A whitewashed crow soon shows black again.

Dangerous enemies will meet again in narrow streets.

Four things come not back: the spoken word, the spent arrow, the past life, and the neglected opportunity.

Hold back some goods for a thousand days and you will be sure to sell at a profit.

Never do anything standing that you can do sitting, or anything sitting that you can do lying down.

He has too many lice to feel an itch.

I dreamed a thousand new paths. I woke and walked my old one.

Of all the thirty-six alternatives, running away is the best.

Govern a family as you would cook a small fish—very gently.

It's your own lantern; don't poke holes in the paper.

Man must be sharpened on man, like knife on stone.

One cannot manage too many affairs; like pumpkins in water, one pops up while you try to hold down the other.

Slander cannot destroy an honest man: when the flood recedes the rock is there.

The beginning of wisdom is to call things by their right names.

The Yangtze never runs backward; man recaptures not his youth.

JAPAN

Don't rejoice over him who goes, before you see him who comes.

Never trust a woman, even if she has borne you seven children.

Being lucky is like having a rice dumpling fly into your mouth.

Better to be a crystal and broken than a tile on the housetop.

If you wish to learn the highest truths, begin with the alphabet.

If you have too many boatmen, the boat will end up on the mountain top.

If man has no tea in him, he is incapable of understanding truth and beauty.

Deceive the rich and powerful if you will, but don't insult them.

If a man be great, even his dog will wear a proud look.

Don't stay long when the husband is not at home.

If you understand everything, you must be misinformed.

Never rely on the glory of the morning or the smiles of your mother-in-law.

A pig used to dirt turns its nose up at rice.

A good husband is healthy and absent.

Even a Buddha will lose his composure if asked something too many times.

Poke around in a bush and a snake will come out.

If three women visit, expect noise.

Even monkeys fall from trees.

Fear earthquakes, thunder, fires, and fathers.

KOREA

A kitchen knife cannot carve its own handle.

You will hate a beautiful song if you sing it too often.

MALAYSIA

A lost wife can be replaced, but a lost reputation means ruin.

A crime leaves ripples like a water beetle, a trail like a snail, and a reek like a horse-mango.

He can see a louse as far away as China but not the elephant on his nose.

An ox with long horns will be accused of butting, whether it's guilty or not.

The existence of the sea means the existence of pirates.

Smack a tray of water and you get to wash your face.

Don't use an ax to embroider.

The turtle lays thousands of eggs without anyone knowing, but when the hen lays an egg the whole country is informed.

THAILAND

Don't make the bamboo water containers before you see the river.

In the town where people wink, you must also wink.

UNITED STATES

A tree never hits an automobile except in self defense.

If you can't ride two horses at once, you shouldn't be in the circus.

An American will go to hell for a bag of coffee.

Honesty is like an icicle; if once it melts, that is the end of it.

Cemeteries are full of people who thought the world couldn't get along without them.

In politics, a man must learn to rise above principle.

Never be content with your lot. Try for a lot more.

Never trouble trouble till trouble troubles you.

When pleasure interferes with business, give up business.

ARGENTINA

Children's love is like water in a basket.

If you have a tail of straw, then keep away from the fire.

BELIZE

Don't call the alligator a big-mouth till you have crossed the river.

CHILE

A husband at home is like a flea in your ear.

HAITI

If work were good for you, the rich would leave none for the poor.

The goat which has many owners will be left to die in the sun.

If you want your eggs hatched, sit on them yourself.

If someone sweats for you, you change his shirt.

The pencil of God has no eraser.

JAMAICA

If you saw what the river carried, you would never drink the water.

Make a friend when you don't need one.

MEXICO

A person born to be a flower pot will not go beyond the porch.

Bad weeds never die.

NATIVE AMERICAN

It's impossible to awaken a man who is pretending to be asleep.
Navajo

Beware of the man who does not talk, and the dog that does not bark.
Cheyenne

There is nothing as eloquent as a rattlesnake's tail.
Navajo

If you see no reason for giving thanks, the fault lies in yourself.
Minquass

Do not judge your neighbor until you walk two moons in his moccasins.
Cheyenne

Walk lightly in the spring; Mother Earth is pregnant.
Kiowa

Man has responsibility, not power.

Tuscarora

Don't let yesterday use up too much of today.
Cherokee

Force, no matter how concealed, creates resistance.
Lakota

The bird who has eaten cannot fly with the bird that is hungry.
Omaha

All plants are our brothers and sisters. They talk to us and if we listen, we can hear them.
Arapaho

In age, talk; in childhood, tears.
Hopi

White men have too many chiefs.
Nez Perce

There are many good moccasin tracks along the trail of a straight arrow.
Sioux

RITUALS

BIRTH

LABOR PAINS

Among the Sia, a native people of New
Mexico, the midwife acts out the
process of labor. In addition, the father
of the woman preparing to give birth
burns a ritual fire, dips eagle feathers in
the ashes, throws the ashes to the four
directions, and then, using the feathers,
draws ash down the mother's body.
And if that isn't enough, the woman's
sister-in-law places an ear of corn near
the mother's head, and blows on it
during contractions to help the baby
out of the body.

PLACENTA RITES

The placenta is revered in many societies. Having
guarded the baby before birth, it will continue to do
so in life. The placenta may be burned or buried with
all the ceremony attached to the funeral rites of a
person—even as a spiritual mother or sibling to the
baby. In the Philippines the placenta is hidden in a
bamboo tube and hung in or near the house to guard
against evil.

In Bali this reverence is extended to all the
accompaniments of birth: placenta, blood, amniotic
fluid, and the umbilical cord. They are viewed as the
baby's brothers. Before any form of sibling rivalry can
occur, the placenta is buried in a small shrine, and
prayers are said to it daily.

DEATH

Several thousand years ago, the Egyptians had developed techniques of preserving, after a fashion, the bodies of the noble or wealthy:

The first step was to remove the brain of the dead person and to fill the skull cavity with resin. Then the internal organs were removed through a hole cut in the abdomen. They would be washed in spices and either returned to the body or stored in jars that were buried alongside the body. The body was immersed in natron (a sodium compound and natural preservative) for up to ten weeks. Then the body was cleaned and dried in the sun. Over 1,000 yards of bandages were used to wrap the body, before finally it was placed in its sarcophagus.

In ancient Egypt, the bodies of the dead would be turned around several times after burial, so that the spirits would be confused and could not find their way back to the body or the land of the living to haunt them.

KOREAN DEATH RITES

The Korean who dies away from his or her home is traditionally believed to wander forevermore as an unhappy ghost. Therefore, no matter how frail or sick, a person who is believed to be near to death is liable to be dragged home, no matter how far they must go.

After death, hair combed from the head of the corpse and clippings from its nails are gathered and placed in five small wallets, which are interred with the body. Three spoonfuls of rice are inserted into the corpse's mouth, together with coins. This rice and money eases the journey of the dead person into the afterlife. The corpse is clad in special cloth and then seven turns of rope are bound tightly around it. Only then is the body ready to be placed in the coffin.

AVOIDING SPIRITS

The Navajo would burn the body of the dead person, as well as his hut. The mourners would take a roundabout route to get home, so that the spirit of the departed person could not follow them. Once home, the friends and relatives would stand in the smoke of a fire to purify themselves.

FRANCE

In some cultures there is an emphasis on destroying all traces of the dead so that there can be no harmful lingering influence on the world of the living. In France it was once the custom to burn the straw on which a person had lain when dying as well as their clothes (a foresighted precaution to prevent the spread of disease), while neighbors and kin jumped through the flames singing.

FOOD FOR THOUGHT

Disposing of the dead by burying them in the ground to be corrupted and consumed by worms is a practice that many cultures regard with horror, whereas cremation is viewed as purifying and wholesome. But even this is regarded as wasteful of the precious element of fire by Parsees. They return their dead to the cycle of existence by a more direct route. In Iran and India—even in the heart of the bustling modern city of Benares—stand the Towers of Silence, wooden platforms on which the bodies of the recently deceased are laid, to be consumed by vultures.

MAKING A SNOWMAN

Some Inuit (Eskimo) peoples built a small igloo over the body of a dead person, making a sort of snow tomb.

FAT BURNING

In Irian Jaya, which occupies the western half of New Guinea, the Dani people cover a newly dead man's body with pig fat. This makes it burn vigorously in the cremation fire. Arrows are fired into his body to release his spirit to travel to the afterlife. A sacrifice is demanded of a young girl of his family: one joint of a finger, which is hacked off with a stone axe and thrown into the funeral fire. Her loss will be a reminder to everyone of the dead man for as long as she lives.

A DEAD MARRIAGE

In Romania, an unmarried woman who dies is traditionally given a "wedding of the dead" on burial, so that her unsatisfied spirit does not return to bother the living. A man plays the role of the groom and takes vows by the coffin. Family and friends play the roles of bridesmaids, and a doll is placed in the coffin to represent the children she didn't have.

INCOGNITO

The Tiwi of Bathurst Island, in northern Australia, believe funerals are thronged with evil spirits. The participants at the funeral paint themselves and cut their hair at the ritual so that they go unrecognized.

NEVER MISSING A GAME

Certain peoples of Madagascar dig up the bones of the recently dead after the skin has rotted away. While the skin is there, the person's spirit cannot cross to the spirit world. The family wash the bones, and then take them to some favorite event of the deceased, such as a dance or a football game. The bones can be finally returned to the grave, in the knowledge that the spirit has gone to the afterlife. It certainly gives new meaning to the phrase "family outing."

The Maoris of New Zealand treat the bones of the dead in a similar way. However, they have a distinctive pre-burial ritual. The corpses of the deceased are propped in a sitting position, clad in fine clothes. The whole village views them like this, while mourning and cutting themselves with knives. The hut in which this takes place is later burned.

GOOD GRIEF

Unrestrained expressions of grief are normal throughout the non-Western world. In Britain, however, for many years it was believed that excessive tears held back the departing soul, and that one should not weep for at least three hours after a death.

HUMAN SACRIFICE

AZTEC GRATITUDE

The Aztec civilization of pre-Columbian America was centered around the practice of frequent large-scale human sacrifice. The sides of its pyramidal temples were washed with the blood of the sacrificial victims, who included the most prized among the community's young men and women, or the best specimens among the captured warriors of enemy nations. In this way the Aztec people repaid their debt of gratitude to the sun-god, whose children they believed that they were.

One Aztec rite was devoted to the earth-goddess: the victim was expertly flayed and his skin was worn by the priest. The god of fire, appropriately enough, received his tribute in the form of victims burned alive. The victims sacrificed to the supreme god were prisoners of war, whose living hearts were torn from their bodies.

In one such festival the victim was a prisoner who spent a whole year in preparation. He took the name of the god to whom he was to be sacrificed, and was given four high-born girls as wives. He lived in honor until the day of his sacrifice came, when, at the top of the sacrificial pyramid, a priest tore his heart out.

GREAT EXPECTATIONS

The funeral of an important or respected person was often accompanied in the past by the sacrifice of others of lower status. In ancient Egypt and China, the wives of a great man who had died, or at least those of them who had not borne children, were killed and buried alongside him, together with rich and rare possessions.

SUTTEE

In India the practice of *suttee* continued until British rulers outlawed it in the nineteenth century. Traditionally, when a man died, his wife, dressed in her finest clothes, had to mount his funeral pyre and take her place beside him before the torch was put to it.

SLAVE TRADE

In Japan, two or three dozen slaves would be dispatched to accompany some great man in his journey after death.

MARRIAGE AROUND THE WORLD

PIECE OF CAKE

In Japan newlywed couples cut their wedding cakes with swords.

PLATES

In northern England it was once the custom to toss a plate that carried a wedding cake over the bride's head as she left the church. The greater the number of pieces that the plate shattered into, the better the omens for the marriage.

TOOTHY GRIN

In Bali, the bride and groom have their teeth filed at their wedding, by the officiating priest. A person who dies before they are married has his or her teeth filed before the cremation.

INDIAN OCEAN

A traditional-style marriage ceremony on the island of Madagascar in the Indian Ocean may not be for you, unless you're very fond of beef. A cow is slaughtered during the proceedings and all the guests have to drink its blood.

INDIA

Boys and girls of the Gujar ethnic group in India get married at the age of seven. The ceremonies are dedicated to Ganesha, the elephant-headed god. Twice a day for eight days the boy and girl march in procession through the streets. The day before the wedding the boy rides on horseback to his bride's home. He is accompanied by an entourage of 100 friends and relatives, and he is adorned with garlands of bank notes.

After the marriage ceremony the bride and groom ride together in a bullock cart to the groom's home, where the bride lives for three days. She then returns to her family and rejoins her husband when she reaches puberty.

POLYNESIA

In the Marquesas Islands in Polynesia, the newlywed couple departs from the ceremony over a human carpet of the bride's relatives.

CAJUNS

Among the Cajuns of the southern United States, when a woman is married before her older sisters, those sisters will dance on washtubs at the wedding, while making sweeping actions with their brooms. This little piece of self-mockery highlights to all the eligible men that they are still available.

MARRYING ROYALTY

The chance to marry a king is not a hopeless dream in Swaziland. In fact, as many as 20,000 girls dance before him each year, hoping to be chosen as his bride. King Mswati III, the present king, may marry as many women as he chooses; his father, King Sobhuza II, married more than 60 women.

SOUTH AFRICA

In South Africa, the traditional way for the happy couple's families to have fun at the wedding is to sing insulting songs about each other.

MARRIAGE EN MASSE

Multiple wedding ceremonies are popular in many places, but the world record for marrying in a crowd must surely go to the Rev. Sun Myung Moon's Unification Church, better known as the Moonies.

It is vitally important to the Unification Church that Moon's followers marry among themselves and have children. Accordingly, the Church tells followers whom they should marry, and most comply. The five-step Blessing Ceremony has certainly succeeded: in 1960 the Marriage Blessing was given to three couples in Seoul, Korea; in the following year 33 couples took part; in 1998, it is claimed that 120 million couples took part globally via satellite TV.

ANIMAL MARRIAGE

DONKEYS

Sometimes in India a marriage will be arranged
between donkeys in the hope that it will bring
rain. The ceremony is an ancient one, described
in the Hindu scriptures. One such ritual was held
in June 2003, at a temple in the city of Bangalore.
The bride, called Ganga, wore a green sari,
bordered with gold. The groom, called Varuna,
wore a white dhoti, or loincloth. Guests feasted,
and then the donkeys were led in procession
through the streets.

CANINE NUPTIALS

When a child's first tooth appears on the upper gum,
the child is believed to be in grave danger. Only
marriage to a dog can provide the answer. In June
2003, a nine-year-old girl from the Santhal tribe in
West Bengal married a stray dog in an elaborate
ceremony. The girl's future marriageability was not
adversely affected: she can marry any man of her
choice in the future.

PACHYDERM PUBLICITY STUNT

Two pairs of elephants went through a wedding ceremony in the
city of Ayutthaya in Thailand on St. Valentine's Day in 2001. One
couple consisted of Sweetheart and Blossoming Lotus; the other
two animals were Honey and Golden Tusk. The ceremony, which
was held at a department store, was not too serious: its purpose
was to publicize Thailand's national animal, the elephant, whose
numbers are declining at present.

RELIGIOUS FESTIVALS

There is a game in which a goose is blindfolded and girls make a circle around it. Whoever the goose touches first will be the first to get married.

Ivy can be used to foretell the good or bad fortune of the coming year. For each person whose fate you are interested in, put one green ivy leaf into a bowl of water on New Year's Eve. If it is still green on Twelfth Night Eve, that person will be blessed with good luck. If it has become spotted, it foretells illness. The locations of the spots show the skilled diviner which part of the sufferer's body will be affected by the illness. If the leaf is spotted all over, the victim of the illness will die.

Halloween is said to be derived from the pagan Celtic festival of Samhain, on which the souls of the dead were believed to revisit the earth. "Trick or treat" may be descended from a custom of offering food to the wandering spirits.

Leaves can be used to foretell a person's health at Halloween, according to a variant of a similar leaf-divination tradition used at Christmas. Each person places an ivy leaf in a bowl of water overnight. If the leaf bears a coffin-shaped mark the following morning, that person will die within 12 months.

EASTER IN THE PHILIPPINES

Every Easter, Christ's Passion is reenacted in the village of Barangay, in the Philippines. A procession of dozens of hooded men with bare backs beat themselves with bamboo sticks, and occasionally are beaten by someone else with a wooden mallet in which are embedded fragments of glass. Sometimes they lie on the ground to receive blows from attendants. Blood spatters the onlookers as the whippings proceed. This part of the festival ends when the flagellants have their wounds dressed, remove their hoods, and stroll home.

LIFTING

An old English custom was that of "lifting," carried out on Easter Monday and clearly related to the Resurrection of Christ. The young men of the locality would lift a chair shoulder-high, bedecked with ribbons and carrying a damsel chosen from among the local girls. They would then carry the chair in procession. The following day it would be the turn of the young women to lift a favored young man in the same way.

ENGLAND

A peaceful custom has long existed in England, and is zealously preserved in some villages today. On Easter Sunday, smartly dressed children form a complete circle around a church, with their backs to the building. They move on to the next church to do the same thing again.

THE EXPLODING CART

One of the strangest of all Easter ceremonies takes place in Italy. A ceremonial cart draws up before the Basilica of St. Maria del Fiore of Florence, and a wire is run from the cart to the great altar inside. A firework shaped like a bird and called *la columbina* (the dove), is hung on the wire at the altar, and ignited. The rocket speeds along the wire and hurtles into the cart. The cart's freight consists of a vast number of fireworks of all descriptions, which explode spectacularly. The better the display,

EGGS IS EGGS

In Belgium the traditional hiding place for Easter eggs is in gardens. The children who search for them are told that church bells lay the eggs. In Yugoslavia, eggs are dyed black and placed on family graves. Eggs are colored a joyous red in Greece and Romania. When friends meet on Easter Sunday, they knock eggs together, and one cries, "Christ is risen!" while the other responds, "He is truly risen!"

UKRAINE

In the Ukraine people put painted eggs on graves and cover them with earth. If in the morning the egg is undisturbed, the soul of the dead person is at peace. If the earth has been disturbed, the soul is not at peace and prayers need to said for the deceased.

JUDAS BEATING

Easter is a time when effigies of Judas are beaten, hung, and burned in the streets of Mexico. Sometimes in place of the effigy of Christ's betrayer, a paper mache piñata is beaten with sticks. It is filled with candies, which eventually spill out when it breaks open at the feet of the children.

PRE-CHRISTIAN TIMES

Eggs have been associated with spring, the season of new birth and awakening, from pre-Christian times. The peoples of the Middle East and of ancient Greece and Rome all exchanged eggs as gifts at their springtime festivals.

PAGAN FESTIVALS

HOT LUCK

Festivals of fire are held at midsummer in many cultures. One ritual involves sending a blazing wheel coursing downhill. It is said to represent the sun's descent in the sky from its highest point at the summer solstice to its lowest at the winter solstice. It is believed that it is good luck if the wheel keeps burning all the way down, but if the fire goes out before the wheel reaches the bottom of the hill, a bad harvest is presaged.

ROAST MEAT

In many European countries, cattle and pigs were traditionally put through a sort of ordeal by fire at midsummer, and were driven through flames. This purified them of harmful influences and ensured that they would be healthy and fertile in the coming season.

FIRE

People, too, have gone through fire rituals that seem to be memories of what would have been terrible ordeals in earlier societies. People would jump over the bonfires, jumping as high as they could to promote the health of the crops. In North Africa childless couples would jump the fires so that they would have children; but in France women early in pregnancy would do so in order to ease their labor. In Ireland and elsewhere unmarried girls would jump the fires to guarantee that they would win a husband; but in France they would run round the fires nine times to obtain the same outcome.

ASHES TO ASHES

The by-product of the fires had their own magical efficacy. The ashes, placed in hen's nests, would encourage the laying of eggs. If they were mixed with cattle's drinking water, the herd would thrive.

SOLSTICE FESTIVAL

In Belarus, the solstice festival, the most popular in the calendar, is known as Kupalle. Nowadays this name is said to be taken from a Christian saint called Ivan Kupala, although in pre-Christian times the name was traced to a lunar goddess, Kupala.

KUPALLE FIRES

The fires that are lit on Kupalle night have magical powers. If you burn flax plants in the fires and sing a special chant, you can make the crops flourish. Coals from the fire can be scattered among crops to promote their health. And, as in other countries, cattle are driven through the fire to purify them. Children can be brought close to the fire to bring them spiritual well-being, and the clothes of the sick can be dried on the fire to bring health.

There are various types of fortune-telling on Kupalle night. Girls can float wreaths of flowers on the river, and the ones whose wreaths get entangled with other plants can look forward to early marriage. If a plantain leaf is picked at a crossroads and placed under a pillow, it will bring dreams of a future spouse. If a couple can see the flower of a fern magically glowing, as it does on Kupalle night, they will live happily and, better still, would have the gift of foreseeing the future. On that night, too, trees can talk and walk from place to place.

THE SATURNALIA

Every year, on December 17, ancient Rome would give itself over to seven days of orgy called the Saturnalia. The festival was named after the god Saturn, who had once been a king of Italy and had taught the people the arts of agriculture as he presided over a golden age of peace, equality, and virtue. During the Saturnalia the Romans decked their homes with evergreens and exchanged gifts.

The most amazing feature of the Saturnalia was the total reversal of the roles of menials and their social superiors. In each home, the servants could say whatever they wished and behave as they wished, completely safe from punishment. At meals they could eat and drink as they liked and their masters would even wait on them at table.

HINDUISM

MAKING BOYS INTO MEN

MAKING BOYS INTO MEN

A boy of the Brahmin caste makes the transition into *brahmacharya*, the "disciplined living" of adulthood, in an elaborate ritual. Traditionally, he is sent to a special residential school, which may be a monastery. One of the names for this separation from home is "half-marriage." Before his departure he must learn certain Hindu rituals, must overcome his attachment to his mother, and must learn symbolic begging. His sisters bathe him. His head is shaved all over and he is decorated with ritual dyes and garlands, and goes through a ceremony to bring him into bachelorhood. He then begs symbolically from the guests, who respond with gifts.

INSTANT DUNG

One of the Hindu purification rituals requires the use of cow dung. An enterprising company in Calcutta (Kolkata) is now selling instant dung. The user just needs to add water to give the dung the needed consistency. Camphor, turmeric and sandalwood are included in the material to make the dung less offensive.

DIWALI

The festival of Diwali is also called the Festival of Lights. It falls on variable dates during July or August. It occurs at the end of the monsoon season. The monsoons bring insects and the threat of rot and mold in homes, so houses must be meticulously cleaned, perhaps repainted, and then decorated to make them bright and welcoming. Only if the house is attractive will Lakshmi, the goddess of good luck and wealth, wish to visit. If she does not, it will be visited instead by her brother, bringer of bad things. During the five-day festival everyone wears their best clothes, friends and neighbors visit each other and sumptuous meals are eaten. There are firework displays at night, and candles are floated on the rivers in little boats.

BUDDHIST KALACHAKRA INITIATION

THE WHEEL OF TIME

As part of their progress toward enlightenment, Buddhist monks participate in a great ritual called the Kalachakra Initiation. Kalachakra is a deity whose name means "Wheel of Time," which is the great cycle of birth and rebirth that Buddhists believe all living things go through on their way toward enlightenment. The core of the ritual is the construction, contemplation, and destruction of a great circular picture called a mandala, representing the Wheel.

The destruction of the mandala symbolizes the Buddhist view of the impermanence of all things. The Vajra Master, or ritual leader, cuts through the mandala with a ritual implement, the monks gather up the sand and it is ceremonially placed into some nearby body of water, mixing the peace of Kalachakra with the world. The ritual and the mandala have traditionally been kept strictly secret from those other than Buddhist monks. But in recent years the Dalai Lama, wishing to improve the world's understanding of Tibetan Buddhism, has presided over the ceremony and let others view the mandala, before it is destroyed in the customary way.

INDIGENOUS PEOPLES

PENTECOST ISLANDERS

The youths of Pentecost Island invented the prototype of
bungee jumping centuries ago. It makes the modern Western
form of the sport look wimpy. The divers of Pentecost Island
leap above land—admittedly, soft ground—that has been
dug over immediately before the ritual begins. The jumper's
fall is sharply broken by almost non-elastic vines tied around
his ankles. Only the experienced judgment of a tribal elder
assures him that the vine will hold and not snap.

The Pentecost Island land-divers perform their ritual around
harvest-time, which is usually in May. They believe that the
higher the jumps they make, the better their crops will grow.

Like all good rituals, land-diving has its legendary origin.
Although the practice is now confined to men and boys, it is
supposed to have begun with a woman. Fleeing her angry
husband, she climbed a high tree, but he followed. Then she
leaped, but he jumped after her. Unknown to him, she had
been wise enough to tie lianas around her ankles, and she
lived while he died.

STAGES IN THE MASAI LIFE

Before boys can be circumcised, they must go through a pre-circumcision ceremony. One boy is chosen to be the chief of his age-set. This is a misfortune for him, because he is regarded as having taken on his peers' sins. The ceremony itself involves day-long dancing.

When the boys reach puberty, it is time for circumcision. For seven days beforehand the boys herd cattle. On their way to the ceremony they are at turns encouraged and taunted by men and other boys: in mocking songs they are told that if they run away or struggle against the knife, they will be killed or cast out of the tribe. No pain-killers are used in the operation and the effects take months to heal. After the ceremony, the boys receive gifts of cattle, and having become men, are permitted to carry a warrior's spear, to tend large herds and to travel alone at night.

Later in life, having graduated to the status of a senior warrior, he goes through the meat ceremony. A bull is slaughtered and consumed. Then it is necessary for wives to prove to their husbands that they have not been unfaithful with men from a younger age-set. (It is perfectly all right for a wife to have lovers among men of the same age-set.) The warriors establish this by wrestling matches among themselves. How close they can come to the hide of the slaughtered bull determines how fortunate they have been. When a wife is judged to have been unfaithful, she must buy her way back into her husband's favor with a cow given by her family.

CANNIBALISM

Cannibalism is an honored tradition in many cultures. It was even known among the ancient Greeks. According to the historian Herodotus, the Calations, considered it a duty to consume their revered kinsfolk when they died.

ASHES

A variant was practiced by one
Queen Artemisia, who mixed the
ashes of a dead lover with wine,
and drank it.

AUSTRALIAN ABORIGINALS

Australian aboriginals used to eat slain enemies, and also their dead
kinsfolk. There were very strict rules specifying which relatives were
permitted to eat someone.

When someone died, a man would wrap the body in bark and leave it
till the morning. Male cousins—specifically, sons of the dead person's
maternal uncles—did the cooking. Bark would be laid over hot stones,
the body placed on that and another layer of bark put over the
corpse. When the body was sufficiently cooked, it was removed from
the ground, laid on bark, and cut up.

Men, women and children in the permitted groups were allowed to
take part in the feast, and enjoyed it. Then the bones of the deceased
were wrapped in bark and placed on a tree platform. The camp had
to move immediately to a new location, because the frightening spirit
of the dead person would haunt the old location to see that all the
ceremonies were properly carried out. Only when they were
completed would it be free to leave to return to its original home.

After some months men of the correct grouping would take the
bones, now clean after exposure to the weather, from the platform.
The arm-bones would be wrapped in bark and handed to the mother.
She would cradle them and wail all day and night. It might be several
years later that the bones were taken back from the mother and
placed in a decorated log coffin. After many complex rituals, the coffin
was finally placed among rocks on a hillside, or placed in the
branches of a tree, and was left for nature to take its course.

CANNIBALS DISGUSTED BY CANNIBALISM

One of the last peoples to be forced to give up cannibalism is the Wari' tribe of Amazonia. The outside world had no dealings with them prior to the 1950s. Until recently it was their practice to eat the bodies of their deceased relatives and enemies whom they had vanquished.

BODY COUNT

Jean de Léry, a sixteenth-century missionary, recorded that the natives of Brazil were honored by their peers for their acts of cannibalism. After a cannibal feast, they would return to their homes, make cuts in their arms, chests and thighs, and rub black powder into them to make them into permanent scars. The highest respect went to men with the greatest number of scars on their bodies.

EATING YOUR OWN

Eating dead enemies was a way of triumphing over them, and perhaps fits the idea of cannibalism that has long prevailed in the West. Cannibalism of dead kin was a way of healing the grief of the survivors, and giving the dead a decent exit from the world. Nowadays the Wari', whose numbers are down to 2,000, bury their dead as the authorities compel them to do. They say they find it hard to accept the thought of their loved ones' bodies decaying in cold, wet soil.

SCAR FACE

Another missionary recorded slightly different customs in another tribe. Here the scarring preceded the cannibalism. And the business of making the scars and recovering was a full-blown ritual, with the man spending days not moving from his bed while the scars healed.

HUMAN SACRIFICE

Fiji is associated with a dark past of human sacrifice. When a temple or chief's house was built, victims were buried alive to "hold up" the building, as they described it. When war canoes were launched, it was over the bodies of living victims, giving the craft a baptism of blood. The victims were cooked and eaten afterward.

RITES OF PASSAGE

NATIVE AMERICANS

A major ceremony among many tribes was the Sun Dance, a summer ritual lasting several days. There would be fasting, sacrifices, prayers, dancing, and singing. With some tribes, wooden skewers would pierce the participants' chests, and thongs would connect the skewers to a central pole, around which the men would dance until the skewers broke free of the flesh. The pain and the exhaustion involved in this ceremony could induce ecstatic visions in the participants.

SPIRITUAL VISIONS

Among Native American tribes boys entered into flourishing manhood only when they had been visited by a vision from the spirit world. The vision would be in the form of an animal or bird and for the rest of his life would become that person's personal totem: that is, would be in a special relationship to him, a sort of mystical brotherhood. The boy who failed to see a vision was destined for an ignominious and impoverished life.

NIGERIA

The Ohafia people of southeastern Nigeria recognize one stage in a boy's transition to manhood around the age of seven. The boy is given his first bow and arrows then, and he is expected in due course to kill a small bird with them. When he does so, he parades through his village in ceremonial clothes with the bird tied to the end of the bow, singing triumphant songs, which include plenty of derision aimed at his age-mates who have not yet equaled his feat.

ITALY

A boy on the eve of puberty is traditionally put through a ritual intended to bless his later life. He is passed between the two halves of a split sapling, three times. Inside the sapling is a small picture of the Virgin Mary. The halves of the sapling are tied together, with the picture inside, so the Virgin will watch over him.

MODERN CULTS

BLOOD RITUAL

The Aum Shinrikyo cult, which began in Japan in the 1980s,
worshipped its founder, Shoko Asahara, as a god. Asahara's
followers made tea by boiling his beard clippings in water
and would ceremonially drink his blood from small glasses,
sold to them at $7,000 per dose. The worship by his
followers strengthened him to the point where he
encouraged his cult to mount a nerve-gas attack on the
Tokyo subway in March 1995: 5,500 people were affected,
and 12 of them died. On the road to this crime, Asahara had
stoked the devotion of his followers with ever more
extravagant practices.

SPIRITUAL PUSH

The Aetherius Society is a flying-saucer religion that,
according to its literature, has time and again saved the
world from the machinations of enemies in outer space and
the misguided actions of the human race. The society was
founded in the 1950s by George King, an Englishman who
in May 1954 was told by a disembodied voice, "Prepare
yourself! You are to become the voice of Interplanetary
Parliament." A picture of Jesus and another of George King
(who died in 1997), preside over the weekly meetings of the
society. Among the prayers, taped messages, recorded by
King and by various interplanetary messengers, are played.

The Aetherius Society believes the well-being of the
world depends on spiritual energy stored in 19 mountains
around the world. Nine are in Britain, four in the United
States, and the rest are in Europe, Africa, and Australia.
From 1959 to 1961, in "Operation Starlight," King and
his close companions went on several expeditions up
these mountains in order to place "spiritual batteries"
on their peaks.

THE CULTS OF CARGO

Since the late nineteenth century over a broad swath of the South Pacific, at least 70 different local religions have been created that anthropologists call "cargo cults." Their doctrines vary, but all basically believe that soon a new age of prosperity will commence for their adherents. This age will arrive when the ships, and latterly the planes, that hitherto have brought food and luxuries to the white people, will begin to bring them to the native peoples of the area.

Often they teach that white people have intercepted goods that always were intended for the aboriginal people. To be prepared for that day, the cargo cultists build imitation jetties for ships, clear landing strips for planes, build life-size models of planes to go on them, and erect wooden facsimiles of control towers. They conduct ceremonies to welcome the goods that are always, year after year, about to appear. They don mock headphones and talk into mock microphones, and signal to the sky. It makes perfectly good sense to them: if similar rituals bring goods to the whites, why should they not be equally effective for the native peoples? In the end, they have been vindicated: the cargo cultists are now on the tourist routes, and their rituals now bring in tourist cash.

BURNING MAN

A ritual that was established in 1986 and is still going strong takes place every year in the Nevada Desert, around the beginning of September. People set up "theme camps," with titles such as Lost Vegas or Motel 666. They bring their own food and drink, and share it. They ride over the desert in and on "mutant vehicles" of their own designs, and live in shelters they have built. The week of celebration ends with the burning of a human effigy 40 feet tall. The Burning Man festival has echoes of ancient rituals in which effigies made of straw or wicker were burned—sometimes with sacrificial victims, human or animal, inside them. Such ceremonies have been attributed to the Druids. Versions are kept alive in northern Europe, including Britain, Belgium, France, Germany and Austria.

STRAW MAN

In Aachen, Germany, and in northern France, the ritual takes a slightly different form. A man clad in straw acts the part of the victim. After pulling various pranks and after being chased, he seems to end up on the bonfire. In fact the man inside the costume has contrived to slip away.

GREEN MAN

In a more sinister Austrian ritual, a boy clad in green has to go from house to house, collecting wood for the fire in which, potentially, he will be consumed.

RUSSIA

In Russia the figure involved in fire ceremonies was a dummy made of straw and was dressed in women's clothes. A tree is felled nearby and is decked with ribbons. In this case, however, a separate fire is lit, and the young people jump this, carrying the straw woman with them. On the day following the celebration the straw figure is cast into a nearby stream.

OTHER NON-CHRISTIAN RELIGIOUS RITUALS

TIBET

Every New Year the Buddhist monks of Tibet demonstrate their prowess in creating sculptures illustrating different stories from their voluminous scriptures. Sculptures can be up to 30 feet tall. They are an apt embodiment of the Buddhist view that all things are impermanent, because the sculptures are made of butter.

TAOIST

In late September and early October in Thailand, a nine-day Taoist festival begins to introduce a period of fasting. After five days of street processions and religious ceremonies, feats of endurance begin. On day six, devotees run over red-hot charcoal. On day seven, they run barefoot up and down tall ladders, whose rungs have been replaced with sharp blades.

Then there are two days with further processions through the town, but this time the frenzied worshippers do their utmost to mortify their own and each other's flesh. They stick iron skewers, meters long, into each other's bodies; they hoist each other off the ground by steel hooks piercing their bare flesh. It is claimed that participants come through these ordeals unscathed.

BRITAIN

TWELFTH NIGHT

Englishmen used to go out into the orchards on Twelfth Night (January 5), carrying their weapons and well fortified with drink. They would form a circle around the oldest tree, chant a traditional song, and fire their guns (loaded only with powder not shot) at the tree. They wouldn't be allowed inside until they had guessed what meal was being prepared by the womenfolk. The man who guessed correctly was named King for the Evening, and presided over the merrymaking.

HOBBY HORSE

Bucolic rituals are kept alive in English villages and towns today. In the coastal town of Minehead, in Somerset, May Day (May 1) is celebrated with the help of a hobbyhorse, which is a construction worn by a man and very little resembling a horse, but possessing a rudimentary "mouth" and a rope "tail." This particular hobbyhorse is pretty rowdy, and a great drinker. It starts its activities on the night before May Day, making its way from pub to pub, accompanied by a raucous group of musicians. It is likely to butt or lash with its tail any passerby who doesn't make a contribution to charity on the spot.

At Padstow, not very far away in Cornwall, they also have a licentious hobbyhorse, known locally as the 'obby 'oss, which indulges in very similar antics. It also likes to grab women that it meets and rub soot on their faces; they are assured that this will bring them good luck and fertility.

DRESSING THE WELLS

Derbyshire is probably the part of England where the custom of annual well-dressing is maintained most vigorously. The wells are adorned with ribbons, garlands and floral compositions on Biblical themes. The celebrations originate in rituals of thanksgiving to God from the days when all village life depended on the waters vouchsafed by the wells. In some villages, well-dressing has been brought up to date in the custom of dressing the faucets of the home.

BURNING BARRELS

In the seventeenth century the town of Ottery St. Mary in Devon seems to have felt a need to cleanse its streets of evil. In doing so it began its Festival of Burning Barrels. The barrels are soaked for weeks beforehand in tar. Each is lit outside the local pub that sponsors it, and soon burns fiercely. Then it's lifted onto someone's shoulders and carried around the town, whose streets are crowded with onlookers. Some barrels are carried by women or children; at the end of the evening, heavier ones, weighing well over 60 pounds, are carried by men. It is a matter of great pride to take part, and generations of the same families carry some of the barrels. All this happens on Bonfire Night, November 5, when effigies of Guy Fawkes, who plotted to blow up the king and Parliament in 1605, are being burned all over the country.

THE RANDWICK WAP

The small Gloucestershire village of Randwick has a peculiar custom called the Wap, which is performed early in May. The word "wap" comes from the old "wappenshaw," meaning "weapon showing," but no weapons are in evidence nowadays. A special part of the event is called the "fracas," in which villagers in fancy costumes of the Tudor and Regency periods make a procession from the village war memorial to the Mayor's Pool. Leading the way is the Mop Man, carrying a wet mop which he applies to as many bystanders as come within reach. The mayor and the Festival Queen are carried shoulder-high until they reach the pool, into which the mayor is dunked.

CHEESE-ROLLING

Randwick (see the Randwick Wap, described above) also indulges its eccentricity by engaging in cheese-rolling. The Sunday before the Wap, three large cheeses are rolled counterclockwise around Randwick Church. This is said to ward off evil spirits. One cheese is cut up and distributed to the crowds.

The Randwick obsession with cheese goes further than this. Following the Wap, everyone assembles on a local hill and watches contestants chase a 25-pound cheese as it rolls down the very steep hillside. The same madness is enacted around the same date at nearby Cooper's Hill. The two events between them rack up dozens of serious injuries, keeping the local hospitals busy.

WOOLSACK RACES

The British obsession with running up and down steep hills is in full evidence at Gumstool Hill, Tetbury, in Gloucestershire, at the end of May. That's when teams of four race up and down the one-in-four gradient, carrying sacks of wool weighing 60 pounds (for the men's teams) or 35 pounds (for the ladies' teams). The event is 300 years old and was apparently started as a test of prowess by young cattle drovers.

ST. BRIAVELS BREAD AND CHEESE DOLE

The village of St. Briavels in Gloucestershire displays a sudden loss of decorum on Pentecost each year when the Bread and Cheese Dole takes place. Pieces of bread and cheese are thrown from baskets to crowds waiting to catch them. Recipients dressed in medieval costume are wildly enthusiastic to get the greatest possible share of the offerings. Their costumes are often craftily adapted to this end: wide skirts and broad-brimmed hats are very useful for gathering large quantities of flying food.

STATE OPENING OF PARLIAMENT

At the time of the annual State Opening of British Parliament, the official opening of the parliamentary session for the year, many rituals are in evidence that are connected with the constitutional relationship between the Crown, the House of Lords and the House of Commons. The opening is presided over by the monarch, in crown and regalia, though her authority is now purely symbolic. The opening takes place in the chamber of the House of Lords, once the senior of the two houses of parliament.

The elected Members of Parliament are summoned from the House of Commons to attend on Her Majesty. An official called Black Rod—or in full, the Gentleman Usher of the Black Rod—is dispatched from the House of Lords to summon the MPs. As he approaches the doors of the Commons, they are slammed in his face, as a reminder of the independence of the elected house. He knocks three times on the doors with the ebony cane that gives him his title. Once admitted, he informs the MPs that the monarch awaits them, and then he leads them in procession to the Lords. The peers of the realm (lords and ladies) are already seated, and there is room only for a representative group of MPs to stand in the chamber while they hear the "Most Gracious Speech from the Throne," a statement of the government's program for the coming year, read by the monarch.

GREECE

ROLE REVERSAL FOR A DAY

The Festival of Women is held on January 8, every year in the towns of Monoklissia and Nea Petra. For this one day, it's the women who are looked after by the men. The men stay at home cooking, cleaning and looking after the children. The women meanwhile head off to the cafes, where they drink coffee and ouzo and play backgammon. In the evening, the women enjoy meals prepared by the men in the local tavernas

INDIA

CAMEL FESTIVAL

The importance of camels in the life of Rajasthan, in northwest India, is reflected in the camel festival held every January in the ancient walled town of Bikaner, with its sixteenth-century fort. The major events include camel races, of course, but also "beauty competitions," in which the merits of especially fine beasts are assessed, as in any horse or cattle show. The proceedings begin with a parade in which the cherished animals are put into clown dress.

IRAN

PRAYING FOR RAIN

In Iran, peoples remote from the urban centers still offer rituals, prayers to bring rain when drought strikes. A scarecrow can be paraded around in a dance during the ceremony. And, most bizarre of all, a selected person may be pushed into water to make sure that divine powers get the hint. The lucky victim may be a middle-aged woman, a Seyed (descendant of the Prophet Mohammed), or an identical twin—or, better still, both the twins.

DOWN THE DRAIN

In yet another ritual, women will mix flour and water, climb onto the roof of a mosque, and pour the mixture down the drainpipe, greeting its arrival at the ground with yells and songs.

ITALY

IVREA ORANGE FIGHT

Ivrea lies in the very north of Italy. Its lengthy carnival culminates in three days of mayhem: a battle fought with oranges in the streets of the town, while a bonfire blazes in the square. In the public mind it is linked with Napoleon, who invaded and ruled this area in the early 1800s.

THE FLOWER FESTIVAL OF MONTEROSSO

Once a year the streets of the Italian town of
Monterosso in the Cinqueterre (or Five Lands), of
northwestern Italy are elaborately decorated with
impermanent artworks: pictures created with flower
petals and food items. They can be admired for just
a few hours: then a church procession marking the
Feast of Corpus Domini marches through the
streets—and over the artworks. Still, there's always
the next festival to look forward to in Monterosso: not
just the Festival of Lemons and the Festival of Times
Past but also the Festival dedicated jointly to the
Salted Anchovy and Olive Oil.

JAPAN

TOFU SHRINE

An old Buddhist ritual of Japan takes place every
December. All the broken and bent pins and needles
collected in the household are taken to a special shrine
prepared in the corner of a room. There is a pan of tofu
in the shrine. The broken or bent needles are inserted
into this one by one, while a prayer of thanks is said over
the item for the useful work it has done for the family.
Finally the participants wrap the tofu in paper, and float it
out to sea, where it soon sinks.

THE NAKED MAN FESTIVAL

At Kounomiya Shrine in Inazawa City a man is
selected for the coveted honor of being the center
of attention at the rite. He goes through a ritual of
purification in which he is stripped naked and has
his body hair shaved off. He then runs through
crowds of thousands of men dressed only in
loincloths and sandals. They beat him as he passes.
All the bad luck of the men taking part passes from
them into the naked man when they succeed in
making contact with him, which is why the ritual is
so popular. He carries on like this for at least an
hour before he is carried to the shrine. Here he
takes part in prayer before being allowed to dress
again. He is then chased out of town.

BABY SUMO

Toddlers who have just learned to walk are pitted against
each other in a "crying baby sumo" bout in some places
in Japan. The children wear elaborate sumo wrestling
loincloths and are supported by adults who hold them
and gently push them against each other. It's the first
baby to cry who is the loser, or in some places, who is
the winner. Since in Japan crying is believed to encourage
healthy growth, the whole procedure is a ritualized way of
bringing prosperity to the children; all of whom go home
with a prize.

FIREWALKING AT MOUNT TAKAO

Mount Takao near Tokyo is the home of the Hiwatari firewalking
festival, held in March every year. At the firewalking festival, a huge
bonfire is built and the *yamabushi*, or mountain-dwelling priests,
conduct rituals to drive away evil spirits and expel the sins of the
participants. Pieces of wood that have been rubbed against sick
parts of the body and on which the sufferers' names have been
written are thrown into the fire. When the flames have subsided, the
yamabushi walk on the intensely hot cinders, followed by the other
participants. The ritual will protect them, they believe, from
misfortune through the year to come.

KOREA

PREPARATION FOR BIRTH

In Korea, as is the case in many Asian countries, male children are deeply desired, female ones less so. Rituals have existed since time immemorial to ensure that a new child is a boy. Superstitious women still pray and make offerings over periods of weeks or even months to a host of divinities, including sacred trees and rocks, and even to the stars that make up the Big Dipper constellation. If the mother dreams of fierce animals, it will be a boy. If she dreams of gentle things, such as flowers, it will be a girl.

The grandmother spirit is an important personage to be placated if the birth is to be an easy one and the mother's health assured. And if the future is to be bright for the child, the mother must observe many taboos during the pregnancy. If she eats an excess of duck, the child will waddle like a duck; if she eats too much chicken, the child will have skin like that of a chicken.

AFTER BIRTH

When the child is born, a straw rope across the gate protects the house from evil spirits and ill-intentioned persons. The placenta is burned: in the house if more children are desired; or a distance away if they are not. Delicate foods are offered to the grandmother spirit for seven days after the birth.

Enormous care is taken to protect the child's future well-being. People in mourning or who have taken part in a funeral recently are not permitted to enter the house. In order not to offend the spirits after the birth, or make them jealous of the child, no one praises the child. On the contrary; they gave it humiliating nicknames.

FORTUNE TELLING

The Korean baby is called on to foretell its own future at the age of one. A party is held, and the baby is placed before a low table on which are all manner of gifts from friends. The baby is encouraged to pick one up. If it picks up a pen or ink bottle, it will be a scholar; cakes portend a government career; a toy weapon, the military; money or rice means that it will be wealthy.

MEXICO

RADISH

In Mexico on December 23, the country people hold a curious form of sculpture contest: their medium is the unusual one of the radish. These vegetables are large but of irregular and twisted form. The whole thing celebrates the arrival of the radish in Mexico from Spain. The craftsmen shape the radishes into scenes from the Bible, legend or history, and cash prizes are awarded.

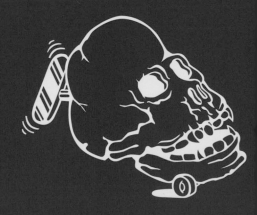

JOYOUS DAY OF THE DEAD

The Day of the Dead is a Mexican festival that has become famous throughout the world. Where most commemorations of the dead in the United States and in most European countries are sad and solemn affairs, the Day of the Dead is an occasion when the spirits of the dead are welcomed back into their old homes and are splendidly entertained.

November 1 is the first day of the festival and is called the Day of the Little Angels, because it is dedicated to children with illnesses. November 2 is dedicated to the adults. Special altars are prepared in private homes, in some part of the house diverted from its normal use. A display is created of mementoes of the loved ones, including some of their cherished possessions, such as a man's pipe, a woman's jewelry, or a child's toy, and photographs of the loved one. A path of rose petals may mark the spirits' way from the street door to the altar. A feast is held, at which there is a place for the spirit, with a bowl of water and a cloth to wash his or her hands, and perhaps tobacco if they were a smoker.

Toys, ornaments, and food are made in the form of light-hearted representations of skulls, skeletons, and coffins. Among the favorite toys are tissue-paper cutouts called *papel picado*. Sugar skulls decorate the altars. A toy skeleton will be found by one lucky person who shares in the round loaf baked especially for the occasion and called the bread of the dead. Sometimes the loaves are in the shape of a body. Much of the bread bought during the festival is intended to be part of the offerings to the dead. The figure of La Muerte, or Lady Death, in various garbs, is to be seen grinning everywhere.

The living also visit the homes of the dead with night-time vigils held in churchyards. The graves are tended and repaired, and then as beautifully ornamented as the domestic altars earlier in the day. Children's graves are gaily decorated with brightly colored ribbons and streamers. Through the night, candles glow in the churchyards, and sometimes there is music and singing, provided by mariachis, or street bands.

The origins of the Day of the Dead are in a pre-Columbian festival dedicated to the dead and to children. That was held in summer, but the Christian Church converted it into a ritual to be held on All Hallows Eve. Today the customs of Halloween, infiltrating from the north, are being increasingly mixed in with those of the Day of the Dead.

SPAIN

TOMATO FESTIVAL

The Grand Tomato Battle of Bunyol is a custom that grew out of a fight in a restaurant in 1945. It was turned into an institution, and is now celebrated each August. The event begins spectacularly, with rockets fired over the town, releasing their payloads of tomatoes onto the crowds below. Then everyone starts flinging tomatoes at each other. After a couple of hours water tankers are sent in to hose down everything and everyone.

SAN BLAS FESTIVAL

San Blas (St. Blaise) was a saint who is honored every year on February 1 in the town of Almonicid del Marquesado. The streets of the town are invaded by 100 men dressed up as devils. The actors are dressed in clothes resembling pajamas and bishops' miters, and each has a huge cowbell on his backside. The devils dance and skip through the streets to the point of exhaustion, and the last devil on his feet is declared the winner.

THAILAND

ENERGETIC VEGETARIANS

The Thai city of Phuket sees a major Vegetarian Festival every year during the ninth lunar month. During this festival period, the pious people of Phuket abstain from meat, alcohol, and sex, but these privations seem to give them extra energy. During the religious processions, the streets resound to the deafening noise of firecrackers dangled in clusters from bamboo poles and thrust at passersby, or thrown around with abandon.

The astonishing ritual at the heart of the festival is cheek-piercing, carried out on hundreds of devotees, both male and female, after they have been put into a trancelike state. Priests drive a heavy metal spike through their cheeks, and then thread some ornamental object through the holes: a string of beads, a skewer, a bunch of flowers.

USA

GROUNDHOG DAY

Ever since Bill Murray starred in a movie of the same name in 1993, the most famous weather ritual in the United States has become much more widely known. The ceremony is carried out on February 2. Punxsutawney Phil, a well-fed groundhog, or woodchuck, named for his home town of Punxsutawney, Pennsylvania, begins the day in his heated burrow on Gobbler's Knob hill. He has been moved there the evening before, having spent the previous year living a pampered life in the Punxsutawney Library. At 7:25 a.m. on Groundhog Day he is hauled out to perform his sole official duty: to find out whether he can see his own shadow. If he can—in other words, if the day is sunny—the rest of winter, up to the spring equinox, will have bad weather. If he can't see his shadow—that is, if the day is overcast—the rest of the winter will be fine.

The ritual at Punxsutawney is now conducted before tens of thousands of people and massed ranks of microphones and T.V. cameras. Punxsutawney Phil is pulled out from under a fake tree stump. The prediction, and its subsequent success, become a matter of public record. It is reported that Punxsutawney Phil's success rate is a meager 39 percent.

BELIEFS

BODILY REACTIONS

Even the twitching of an eye is ominous to the superstitious. A twitching of the left eye foretells a death in the family: of the right eye, more happily, a birth.

An eyelash that has fallen out should be put on the back of the hand; then you should make a wish and throw the lash over your shoulder. But if it sticks to your hand, the wish will not be granted.

ITCHING

If occasionally you get that "burning" sensation of heat in your ears, it means that someone is talking about you: and also, according to some, if your right ear itches, someone is speaking well of you; while if the left one itches, someone is speaking badly of you.

If the bottom of your right foot itches, you are going to take a trip.

Some say that an itching nose portends a visitor. Specifically, if it's the right nostril that is itching, the visitor will be female; if it's the left nostril, the visitor will be male.

If the palm of your right hand itches, you will soon be receiving money. But, as usual, if the palm of your left hand itches, you will soon be paying money out.

Rubbing an itch on wood, or knocking on wood, are believed to be lucky.

SNEEZING

It used to be believed that sneezing could expel your soul. Saying "God bless you!" protected you.

But in the case of a newborn child, the first sneeze was lucky. Until then the child was under the influence of bad fairies, and until that sneeze came was at risk of becoming a witch or warlock.

The omens can become even more complicated when the time of day is taken into account. Some think that it is bad luck to sneeze in the morning before one has one's shoes on. After that, a sneeze before breakfast is lucky, for it means you will receive a gift.

Food and Eating

It is thought that biting your tongue while eating betrays the fact that you have told a lie in the recent past.

A loaf of bread should never be turned upside down after a slice has been cut from it.

Onions are supposed to have healing powers. Cut one in half and place it under the bed of a sick person to cure fever and counter harmful toxins in the patient's blood.

We have all heard that spilling salt is unlucky, and that we must throw a pinch over the left shoulder to neutralize the bad luck. The reason, less well known, is that the devil is waiting there, and throwing the salt will disconcert him for a precious moment while the danger passes.

Salt on the doorstep of a new house will help to protect it against evil.

Spilling pepper portends a serious argument with your best friend.

Formerly, in northern England, parties of people would share a dish of carlins, or cooked peas. When the bowl in the middle of the table was almost empty, the diners would take one pea at a time, in turn. The person who took the last pea would be the next to be married.

Pulling the wishbone, or merrythought, of a chicken is a well known way of getting a wish. Two people make a wish silently as they pull at the bone, and whoever gets the bigger piece will have their wish come true; provided they do not tell anyone what the wish was.

A woman should serve her husband roasted owl if she wants him to be obedient to her every wish.

There's an extraordinary ritual concerning the wishbone for the person who's desperate to know how long she must wait for marriage. A small hole is drilled in the flat part at the angle of the wishbone. She then balances the wishbone on the bridge of their nose, and try to pass a thread through the hole. The number of unsuccessful tries at this task is the number of years he or she will have to wait before marriage.

KNOTS

In West Africa, knotting a piece of grass would be part of a spell that indicated misfortune or death for someone.

An old German cure for warts consisted of tying knots in a piece of string and leaving it hidden under a stone. Whoever trod on that stone would catch the warts, while the original sufferer would be freed of them.

In many countries it is traditionally bad luck to tie any sort of knot during the marriage service; it can result in a barren marriage. Any knot in the clothing of the bride or groom should be undone during the service.

According to Hindu belief, you could be released from fever if a friend could take seven cotton threads to some place where an owl was hooting, and tie a knot at each hoot. Tying the threads around the sufferer's arm was then a certain cure.

Fishermen in the Shetland Islands of Scotland used to buy knotted strings from old women. These strings were believed to have the magical power to control the winds. The more knots a sailor untied, the stronger the winds would blow for him.

LADDERS AND MIRRORS

The unluckiness of walking under ladders has been attributed to the fact that condemned men walked beneath the ladder that led up tho scaffold before they climbed it. Walking under a ladder is supposed to foretell death by hanging. The bad luck can be broken by spitting through the ladder, or else, spitting over your left shoulder immediately afterward.

Other misfortunes have come to be associated with walking under a ladder: for example, an unmarried woman who does it will always be a spinster.

The superstitious believe that a mirror attracts lightning, so that during a thunderstorm it should be covered.

Breaking a mirror is widely believed to bring seven years' bad luck. But it's possible to remedy this disaster. Do not look into the broken mirror, and take the fragments out of the house. Bury the pieces or, better still, wash them in a stream that flows south to counteract the bad luck.

STAIRS AND KNITTING

It is well known that it is bad luck to pass someone else on the stairs. But you should not change your mind and turn around on the stairs: continue up or down as the case may be.

Stumbling when you are going upstairs is good luck—the sign of a wedding coming soon; stumbling when coming down is bad luck.

Knitting a pair of socks for a lover will have unhappy consequences: he will leave you—as could be foreseen from the fact that socks are garments made for walking.

Sticking knitting needles through balls of yarn will bring bad luck to those who later wear the garments made from that yarn.

Do not start to knit clothes for your future children until you are pregnant. To do otherwise will bring bad luck: either you will have no child, or the child will be born sickly.

SHARP THINGS

Inadvertently crossing knives on a table means that there will soon be a quarrel in the house.

Some say that if you drop a pair of scissors, it means your lover is being unfaithful to you. However, if the scissors fall with both points sticking into the floor, it is a lucky omen: it means more work is coming to the household. If only one point sticks in, it means a death is coming.

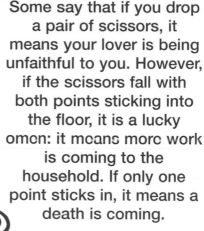

Scissors are regarded as unlucky gifts, because they can cut the ties of friendship or love.

In addition, scissors should never be picked up by the person who dropped them. (A similar belief is held concerning dropped gloves.) If there's no one else around, you can tread on them before picking them up, and ward off the bad luck that way. Be sure to close them before picking them up.

Don't bother to keep searching in vain for some lost item: stick a pin into a cushion, say "I pin the Devil," and you can expect to find the object quickly.

NAILS, COAL, AND HAY

A nail, unlike scissors or mirrors, is considered to be a lucky item. It's lucky, for example, to find one. If you have the good fortune to find one, you can keep it in your pocket as a charm.

Old writers told of curing toothache by scratching the gum of the affected tooth with a new nail until the gum bled. The nail was then driven into a tree.

Hammering a nail into the wood over a door was also believed to protect the people in the house from toothache.

You can find out whether someone is a witch by driving a nail into a footprint they have left. A witch is compelled to return and draw out the nail.

A very widespread belief is that carrying a piece of coal will bring luck. It has always been thought unlucky, when one stirred the fire, to turn the coals over.

Many think it is bad luck to encounter a load of hay while traveling. However, some think it is only seeing the back of the load that is unlucky, and that it is good luck to see the hay approaching you.

COLORS AND BEDS

Red is said to be a lucky charm against illness. For example, the health of a child, who has recently been sick, can be guarded by having him or her wear a red ribbon.

It's bad luck to put a hat on a bed.

If you make a bedspread or a quilt be sure to finish it or marriage will never come to you.

When making the bed, don't interrupt your work, or you will spend a restless night in it.

You must get out of bed on the same side that you get in it or you will have bad luck.

MONEY AND UMBRELLAS

"Find a penny, pick it up,
All day long you'll have
good luck."

"Money on the floor,
More at the door."

If you give a
purse or wallet
to someone, put
a penny in it for
good luck.

Tossing a penny
overboard while on
a sea voyage will
ensure a safe trip.

Some say that it's bad luck to pick up a coin if it's tails side up, but naturally it becomes lucky if it's heads side up.

Opening an
umbrella indoors
is notoriously
unlucky. Opening
the umbrella over
your head
intensifies the
harm.

According to some,
dropping an umbrella on
the floor means that there
will be a murder in the
house in the near future.

Some people believe that borrowing someone else's umbrella is bad luck.

STONES, CRADLES, AND JEWELRY

A stone with a hole in it is lucky. If you find one with two holes, better still. In the past householders often hung them on ribbons over the door, and people would carry them to ward off bad luck in general and rheumatism in particular.

If you rock an empty crib, it will have another occupant before the year is out.

The cradle must be paid for before it enters the house, or the child that lies in it will encounter extreme poverty at the end of its life, and will be buried in an unpaid-for coffin.

Piercing the ears for earrings is widely believed to be good for the eyesight.

To predict the sex of a baby, suspend a wedding ring held by a piece of thread over the palm of a pregnant woman. If the ring swings in an oval or circular motion the baby will be a girl. If the ring swings in a straight line the baby will be a boy.

THIRTEEN, TEETH, AND HAIR

The traditional fear of this number is said to derive from the fact that 13 people were present at the Last Supper. Friday 13th is well known as a day of bad luck, tall buildings often have no floor numbered 13, and there is frequently no room 13 in hotels or hospitals.

Gaps between teeth may not look very nice, but they are a happy omen of prosperity in life—specifically, that one would marry riches.

Dreaming about losing teeth is a sign that some friend or relative will die soon.

Red-haired people have suffered much prejudice in the past. Red hair in a new child was supposed to indicate infidelity by the mother. It is supposed to be unlucky to meet a red-haired person first thing in the morning, and they should not be the first person across the threshold on New Year's Day.

A double crown scalp generally means good luck. The luck can take various forms: some say you are safe from drowning; others that you won't die in the country of your birth; others that you will live in two countries.

Throwing away one's cut hair, or the hair brushed from one's head, is as perilous as parting with anything else from one's body or clothing. Evil spells can be worked against one with the aid of one's hair, or alternatively a bird might use it to make its nest, which will condemn the former owner to constant headaches.

WATER

In England, children suffering from whooping-cough were once taken to the shore at high tide. The ebbing tide was thought to take their cough away with it.

If you make a face (grimace) when the tide is turning, the ugly expression will be forever fixed on your face—just as it will if the wind changes direction.

RIVERS AND DROWNING

To cure stomach pains, gather 12 stones from 12 south-running rivers. If you place these under your mattress at night, they will cure your condition.

Useful information: If you are trying to escape from a witch, try to cross a river — apparently they are unable to cross running water.

The custom of throwing a coin into a fountain to bring good luck is still widespread. But formerly a wide variety of metal objects, from swords to pins and buttons, might be thrown into fountains and wells for the same purpose. Often this would be done as a kind of payment when taking the waters of a well or spring for their curative properties. A well at which this practice was favored would be called a "pin well" or "pen well."

There are magical wells that foretell the future. At Oundle, England, the Drumming Well sometimes predicts disasters by emitting a loud rumble resembling a drum roll. The drying up of a well is usually regarded by local folk as a presage of evil. For example, St. Helen's Well in Staffordshire, England, foretold the outbreak of the English Civil War in 1642 by drying up. Another spring in Northamptonshire gives warning in the opposite way, by overflowing.

HoLY WATERS AND HoLY WINE

The water used in baptism is blessed by the priest. It is thought to have healing powers, but can also be misused by evil spirits or by devotees of Satan. Accordingly, some church fonts have covers that are kept locked when not in use.

On Ascension Day, Heaven was opened to receive the risen Christ. The rain that fell that day was thought to be especially holy, as having come direct from Heaven.

Young girls would once go out on May Day to wash their faces in the morning dew. Not only would the water improve their complexions but the girls had the opportunity to make a wish that they would be married within the year. The most curative dew was gathered from hawthorn, from ivy leaves, or from under an oak tree.

People subject to epilepsy would creep under the communion table three times at midnight to be cured of their fits. Even sweepings from the floor beneath the altar were believed to be efficacious.

CHRISTMAS SUPERSTITIONS

If you eat an apple on Christmas Eve, you will enjoy good health throughout the coming year.

And if you eat plum pudding at Christmas, you will avoid losing a friend before the next Christmas comes around.

Visit plenty of friends at Christmas. In the coming year you will have as many happy months as the number of houses in which you eat mince pies in during this time.

If Christmas Eve is clear, with star-filled skies, the summer will bring good crops.

Leave a loaf of bread on the table after dinner on Christmas Eve. This will ensure there is no lack of bread during the next year.

If you refuse a mince pie when you are offered one at the Christmas dinner, the following day will be marked by bad luck.

A windy Christmas Day is supposed to bring good luck.

The child born on Christmas Day or Christmas Eve is believed in most countries to be especially lucky in its life. However, in Greece they fear that such a child is a wandering spirit. And in Poland they fear that the child may turn out to be a werewolf.

In Ireland it is believed that at midnight on Christmas Eve the gates of Heaven open. Those who die at that time go straight to Heaven, and are spared their stay in Purgatory.

Some people believe that it is bad luck to wear new shoes on Christmas Day.

The wise householder will guard the home's good luck by keeping a fire burning throughout the Christmas season. In fact, it is bad luck to let any fire go out in your house at this time.

Shoes should be placed side by side on Christmas Eve to prevent family quarrels.

Never launder a Christmas present before you give it to someone, as this removes the good luck.

In the Netherlands people believe that if you take a fir stick, thrust it into the fire and let it burn partly, it will serve to ward off lightning if it is put under the bed.

Place a cherry tree branch in water at the beginning of Advent. If it flowers by Christmas, you can be assured to receive lots of luck.

Holly and Ivy must both be included in Christmas decorations. The holly is lucky for the male members of the family, the ivy for the females.

SPECIAL DAYS

The first water taken from a well or spring on New Year's Day has especially strong powers. Such water may bring health, or a good marriage, or general good luck.

If you cut your hair on Good Friday, it is meant to prevent headaches in the forthcoming year.

A child who is born on Good Friday and baptized on Easter Sunday has a mystical gift of healing. If such a child is a boy, he should go into the Church.

One should shed no blood on Good Friday, nor work with wood, nor hammer any nails; the symbolic relationship of all these to the events of the crucifuxion of Jesus is obvious.

Don't start to make a garment on a Friday unless you can finish it the same day; otherwise it will always be unlucky.

Saturday is an unlucky day on which to begin new work. If you do so, you will find that there will be seven Saturdays before its completion. The belief was traditional in many different trades, including servants, farmers, and mariners.

WEDDINGS

The bride shouldn't help to make her own dress. And it is extremely unlucky to tear the dress on the wedding day, or to spill a drop of blood on it. It is unlucky to wear pearls as part of the bridal outfit.

Despite all these hazards, there are plenty of opportunities for the bride to encounter good luck. It's good luck to find a spider in the dress. The marriage is well favored if the bride should meet a lamb or a dove on her wedding day. If she kisses a chimney sweep, she will be lucky, even if he isn't her groom.

Among the bad omens for the wedding day are to see a pig, hare, or lizard running across the road; or an open grave; or meeting a nun or monk (the latter misfortune portends a childless marriage).

Roman Catholics have some extra weapons in their armory to help the success of the wedding. An image of the Virgin Mary placed in a window a week beforehand will help to guarantee a sunny day. Nevertheless if it does rain on the morning of the ceremony, rosary beads hung from a window will help to send the rain away.

There seems to be little agreement about what the weather on a wedding day portends. According to some, raindrops at a wedding mean many teardrops during the marriage. According to others, they simply mean that there will be many children of the union. And others say that rain just means good luck.

If the bride cries on her wedding day, the marriage will never cause her any more tears, supposedly.

A wedding during the time of day when the hour hand on the clock is going upward is lucky; when the hour hand is going downward, it's unlucky.

Traditionally the groom must not see the bride on the day of the wedding before she joins him at the altar. And he should not look over his shoulder to see her as she comes up the aisle to him. Both are considered to augur ill for the couple.

Dropping the wedding ring during the ceremony is a very unlucky omen: some say the marriage is doomed.

Rice thrown as the couple emerge from the church is intended to feed evil spirits, and distract them from disturbing the marriage.

Cans tied to the back of the newly married couple's car will frighten evil spirits away.

To avoid bad luck, the first gift opened by the bride should be the first one she uses.

One tradition says that the person who gives the third gift to be opened will soon have a baby.

The single woman who is a guest at the wedding should take her slice of cake and place it under her pillow. She will then assuredly dream of their future husband.

If ivy leaves representing two lovers are thrown onto a fire, their behavior shows the prospects for the relationship. If they jump together in the heat, the couple will marry; if they jump away from each other, the couple will part.

Stumbling on the threshold when entering the new home is a bad portent. Perhaps the custom of the groom carrying the bride over the threshold is designed to protect against this.

PREGNANCY, TWINS, AND CHRISTENING

If any article of a new baby's clothing is left in the home of a married woman, she will soon become pregnant.

If you want to know the size of your future family, look to see how many Xs you have in the palm of your right hand; that is the number of children you will have.

In Africa it is traditionally believed that twins are unlucky. They may be abandoned to die immediately after birth, and their mother may be killed as a witch.

In Britain it was often thought that if one twin dies, the survivor becomes stronger and acquires healing powers.

It used to be thought unlucky if a child did not cry at its christening. He or she would even be secretly pinched or slapped to make it cry. The reason was that the Devil is driven out at baptism, and will naturally cry out at that moment.

DEATH

There is a grim superstition that babies born during the waning moon will not survive to adulthood.

In ancient times, weapons, utensils, food, and fine clothes would be buried with a corpse so that the deceased would be well provided for in the afterlife. Traces of the custom survived into the twentieth century: A coin was often placed in the mouth or hand of a corpse.

When the soul leaves the body at the moment of death, it is said to be visible as a faint flamelike light. Such corpse-lights or corpse-candles have been reported flickering over the graves of the recently deceased.

If a baby cuts its first teeth very early, it was once thought that it would die when still young.

In other traditions, the lights are seen traveling from the churchyard to the house where someone is about to die. Here they are said to be the souls of the dying person's kin coming to summon him or her to join them.

There is a very widespread belief that it is unlucky to light three cigarettes from one match. This seems to be the modern version of an ancient superstition that it is unlucky to light three candles from a single taper.

When someone dies, all the windows in the room should immediately be opened, to enable the soul of the deceased to make a speedy exit. Furthermore, all doors in the house should be unlocked, for the same reason.

A superstition that goes back to the earliest days of photography states that when three people are photographed together the one in the middle will die first.

It is unlucky to bury a woman in black. She is liable to return to haunt the family.

Generations of children have firmly believed that they must hold their breath while passing a cemetery, lest they breathe in the spirit of someone who has recently died and not yet passed on to the other world.

Cover the mirrors in a house in which there is a dead body: otherwise the next person to see their own reflection will die soon.

Yet another superstition pertinent to the conduct of funerals is: never hold one on a Friday. This portends another death in the family during the year.

It's bad luck to count the cars in a funeral cortege.

It's bad luck to meet a funeral procession head-on.

Nothing new should be worn to a funeral, especially new shoes.

Thunder following a funeral means that the dead person's soul has reached heaven.

It was once the custom in England to ask any visitor to a house where a death had just occurred to view the dead person and touch their corpse. Failure to do so was thought to prevent dreams of the deceased, or encourage possible hauntings.

GHOSTS AND PLANTS

You can protect your home from ghosts by removing a door and hanging it with the hinges on the other side.

Yet another protection is to lay a poker on top of the fire, so that it forms a cross with the top bar of the grate, which will be visible to any evil spirit thinking of entering via the chimney.

The fruit of the mandrake is called the mandrake apple. Held in the hand last thing at night, it induces sleep.

The forked root of the mandrake makes the plant resemble a human figure, and a huge amount of legend and superstition has become associated with the plant. It is supposed to cure sterility and have aphrodisiac powers. It can also help seers to divine the future. Some believe that, while living, it glows in the dark. In addition when pulled from the earth, it utters a shriek that causes anyone who hears it to go mad or drop dead.

An acorn at the window will keep lightning out.

An acorn should be carried to bring luck and ensure a long life.

If you cut an ordinary apple in half and count how many seeds are inside, you will apparently be able to divine how many children you will have.

All clover is regarded as lucky; but the four-leafed clover is, of course, especially so. When you find one, you will be able to see fairies and detect the presence of witches. Traditionally a four-leafed clover would be hidden in cow-sheds or dairies to protect the milk.

Thyme is especially associated with the dead. If the scent of thyme lingers around a place where the plant is not growing, it is a sign that a murder has been committed there.

It is unlucky to give or be given parsley. If your friend wants some from you, let her know that she must take it without your knowledge.

The fern called moonwort has the reputation of loosening anything assembled from iron components. Put into keyholes, it will undo the locks; if horses ride over it where it grows, it will loosen the nails in their horseshoes.

Mistletoe traditionally confers fertility. If a bough of mistletoe was laid next to the first cow that calved in the New Year, it would help the whole herd to multiply.

Some hold that the mistletoe must be burned after Christmas, or else those who have kissed under it will become enemies.

Keep witches at bay by planting rosemary by your doorstep.

Holly is believed to be lucky. Many people keep a sprig of it in the house all year around, not just at Christmas. Keeping a tree growing near a house also provides protection for the inhabitants.

Ivy is lucky for the house it grows on. If the ivy withers, it betokens bad luck.

Birch brings good luck to any house that it decorates, and it was also worn in a buttonhole or on a hat for good luck. It is used to decorate houses on summer festivals, such as Pentecost Sunday or May Day. Crosses made of birchwood defend a house or farm buildings, such as pigsties, against evil spells.

THE MOON

Peasants of Brittany, in northwest France, once believed that a pregnant woman who exposed her skin to moonlight would give birth to monsters.

A tribe in Borneo believes that albinos owe their fair coloring to their father, who is the moon.

More generally, it is widely believed unlucky to point at the moon.

Apples must not be picked when the moon is waning, lest they shrivel up.

Until late into the nineteenth century, the guardians of the royal forests of France were under orders to fell oaks only when the moon was waning, to ensure that the timber was of the best possible quality.

It is believed to be unlucky to see the new moon for the first time through glass. It is also unlucky to see it for the first time on the left hand or over one's shoulder. Plants should be sown with due regard for the phase of the moon. Many kinds of seed should be sown when the moon is waxing (growing); some should be sown just after the full moon.

Sleeping in moonlight was widely believed in Britain to cause blindness, or a swollen face.

Rats will eat poison more readily when the moon is waxing.

Births of animals and people, and marriages, will be unlucky if they occur during the waning moon.

The flow of blood in the human body was once thought to increase with the waxing of the moon. The once-popular practice of blood-letting could be carried out safely only when the moon was waning.

THE STARS

Many think it is just as unlucky to point at the stars as at the moon. And it is also tempting fate to try to count the stars.

You don't have to wait for a shooting star to make a wish. An old rhyme says:

"Star light, star bright,
First star I see tonight,
I wish I may, I wish I might
Have the wish I wish tonight."

ECLIPSES

An ancient Hindu belief is that when the sun or moon is eclipsed, a serpent or demon is eating the heavenly body concerned.

The Chinese ascribed eclipses of both sun and moon to the machinations of a dragon. It was a part of the official duties of mandarins to save the moon or the sun by means of praying, burning incense, lighting candles, and making loud noises on instruments.

Eclipses had a further meaning to the Chinese. If a sovereign were remiss in government, Heaven would terrify him with calamities and strange portents. Eclipses of the sun and moon were "manifest warnings that the rod of empire was not wielded aright."

Christopher Columbus greatly benefited from his knowledge of astronomy and the superstition of the Native Americans. In 1504 he and his men were being kept prisoner by the local people, and were close to starving. He threatened to take away the light of the moon if they did not bring them food. They refused, but were intimidated when on March 1 the moon disappeared as Columbus had foreseen. They brought food and pleaded for his pardon.

BIRDS

The Tower of London has been home to ravens for centuries. It is said that if they ever leave, the Tower will fall and disaster will befall England. The British government takes care that there are always at least six ravens in residence, just to be on the safe side.

When you first hear the cuckoo, you should turn over the money in your pocket. This is supposed to ensure good financial luck throughout the following year.

To hear a bird calling to the north means some serious misfortune involving death or injury; a bird calling in the south signifies a good harvest; one calling from the west is good luck; one calling from the east signifies love.

You should make a wish on seeing the first robin of spring. Make sure you complete the wish before the bird escapes, taking the power of the wish with it.

Having bird droppings land on you or on your nicely polished car is not the misfortune it seems. Many people believe that it is actually good luck.

The croaking of a raven portends death.

Don't be tempted to harm a raven: it might house the soul of the legendary King Arthur, revisiting the world of mortals.

When you see magpies while out walking, an old rhyme tells you their meaning:

"One for sorrow, two for mirth;
Three for a wedding, four for a birth;
Five for silver, six for gold;
Seven for a secret, not to be told;
Eight for heaven, nine for hell;
And ten for the Devil's own self."

According to an old story, a solitary magpie is so unlucky because it was the only bird that refused to enter the Ark with Noah. You can counter this by repeating "Good morning, Mr. Magpie" three times, then asking "How is your wife and family?" when you encounter a single bird.

In some countries in Eastern Europe, to hear the hoot of an owl was very unlucky. To rid yourself of the bad luck and counter any evil spirits, superstition required that you undress immediately, turn your clothes inside out and put them back on.

The owl was regarded by the citizens of ancient Rome as so unlucky that, when one flew into the Capitol in the heart of the city, the whole of Rome had to be purified in a special ceremony.

If you hear an owl hooting and want to counteract the bad luck that this brings, throw peppers, vinegar, or salt into the fire. This will make the tongue of the distant owl sore and it will fly away, leaving you in peace.

A dove or a white pigeon is a fortunate thing to see around someone who is about to die or has just died. It indicates that they will find happiness beyond the grave.

The feathers of the peacock, marked with conspicuous and rather frightening "eyes," are supposed to be very unlucky, particularly if brought indoors.

A nocturnal bird that is seen or heard by day is an unlucky omen.

The Germans used to say that the crossbill would always awaken a child that it found sleeping in moonlight, as this, it was thought, could cause lunacy or death.

DOGS

Dogs are often believed to be capable of seeing ghosts. However, some people believe that only a dog with seven toes can do this.

A black dog crossing your path is considered unlucky in most countries. It's especially unlucky if it follows you and won't be driven away.

If a dog howled outside the house of a sick person, it was thought to be an omen that the person would die. If the dog was driven away and returned to howl again, the omen was thought to be especially bad.

Certain Sioux tribes believed that if a sick person shared their bed with a dog, the illness would be transferred to the animal.

In the past, dogs that had bitten someone were often killed. It was thought that if they were to develop rabies, the same disease would appear in the person they had bitten earlier.

CATS

In the United States, it is unlucky to have a black cat cross your path. It's possible to fend off the bad luck by taking 12 steps backward.

The Irish agreed that the black cat was unlucky; they were even more specific, and said that if it crossed your path by moonlight, you would die in an epidemic.

In the United States it's also traditionally good luck to see a white cat on the road, but bad luck to see it at night. But dreaming of a white cat is lucky.

In Britain, however, it is lucky to see a black cat. In Scotland, it specifically has to be a strange black cat, and on your porch.

On every black cat there is believed to be one white hair. If you can pull that hair from the cat without getting scratched, it will bring you good fortune in wealth and love.

According to an old belief, cats must be kept away from babies because they "suck the breath" of the child.

In Bohemia, the cat was a symbol of fertility. When a cat died it was usually buried in the cornfields to give a good crop.

If an unmarried girl in the South of France steps on a cat's tail, she will meet her future husband within 12 months.

When a girl living in the Ozark Mountains received a proposal of marriage and was uncertain whether to accept, she folded three hairs from a cat's tail into a piece of paper and placed it under her doorstep. The next morning she would unfold the paper to see if the hairs had formed themselves into a Y or N before giving her answer.

When moving into a new home, you should always, according to an American superstition, put the cat in through the window instead of the door, so that it won't leave home and run off.

A cat onboard a ship is considered to bring luck.

French peasants thought they could find buried treasure if they followed a specific ritual with a black cat. They would find an intersection where five roads met, then turn the cat loose and follow it.

In ancient Egypt, cats were revered and were sacred to the goddess Isis. Embalmed cats were buried in the tombs of the great. Surprisingly, a similar sort of reverence may have prevailed in England, thousands of years later, for it was once the practice there to seal mummified cats in the walls of houses to ward off evil spirits.

In England, a cat on top of a tombstone was a sign that the soul of the departed was possessed by the devil.

Sacred cats kept in a sanctuary in ancient Egypt were carefully tended by priests who watched them day and night. The priests interpreted the cats' movements—the twitch of a whisker, a yawn or stretch—to make predictions of events that would happen in the future.

Elsewhere it is believed that if a cat sneezes close to the bride on the morning of her wedding it will be a happy marriage.

According to the Italians, it is good luck to hear a cat sneeze.

According to an American belief, if you see a one-eyed cat you should spit on your thumb, press the thumb into the palm of your other hand, and make a wish. The wish will come true.

TOADS AND FROGS

Perhaps because of its own warty skin, the toad has been regarded as having powers to cure skin afflictions.

Closing a living toad in a bag hung round one's neck and allowing it to die there will cure warts, tumors, and skin diseases.

The toadstone is an undistinguished-looking dark gray or light brown stone that was thought to come from the heads of aged toads. They were carried or worn as lucky charms. They would change color if the owner were bewitched.

A frog brings good luck to any house that it enters.

BATS, MOLES, AND RABBITS

In China and in Poland, bats do not have the ominous connotations that they have in the West: if you see one at an auspicious moment, you can look forward to long life and happiness.

Molehills appearing in a circle around a house portend a death in the family. If they don't form a circle they are luckier, for then they mean only that someone will be moving house soon.

It's said that if a bat lands on your head, it won't get off until it hears thunder.

Moles' feet are a cure-all for toothache and fever in children. They need to be hung around the patient's neck in a bag.

The rabbit's foot is thought to be especially lucky when rubbed on the face of a child. It was formerly often placed in a child's baby carriage. The hare's foot is also regarded as lucky. Actors used to apply their makeup with a rabbit's foot.

A rabbit that crosses the path in front of you bodes well; one that crosses behind you is a bad portent.

MICE, CATTLE, AND SHEEP

Mice were formerly cooked and eaten as cures for colds and fevers. Drinking water in which a mouse had been boiled was also a remedy for quinsy (an inflammation of the tonsils).

To cure a persistent cough, you are recommended to wear a bag around your neck containing a whole nest of mice. Your cough will pass to them and disappear as they die.

The Icelanders say that If the first calf to be born during the winter is white, it presages a bad winter.

It was once thought that by living close to where cows were kept you'd never get tuberculosis.

Carry the bone from a joint of mutton with you as a lucky charm if you wish to ward off rheumatism.

If a child had whooping cough, it could be cured by the breath of a healthy sheep.

Restless sheep are an omen of bad weather.

HORSES AND DONKEYS

Superstitions differ from country to country regarding the lucky or unlucky qualities of white horses. In some places they are lucky, in others the opposite. When you encounter a white horse, you should spit and make a wish. Alternatively, you should cross your fingers until you see a dog.

Some country people still seek to bring luck to their house by leading a horse through it.

Sometimes children would be required to ride a donkey, sitting facing backward, to prevent diseases such as measles.

Letting a black donkey share a field with pregnant mares will guarantee that they foal successfully.

Horse-brasses, which were common before the displacement of the horse by the tractor for working the land, were both ornaments and lucky charms. They took the form of lucky shapes, such as rayed suns or crescent moons.

WOLVES

Many superstitious beliefs gathered around the mysterious and feared wolf. Like other powerful predator animals, it yielded body parts that were especially prized in the pharmacies of the ancient apothecaries. Its liver was held to ease the pain of childbirth. Its paw, kept in a bag around one's neck, could heal throat infections.

One had to be careful riding where wolves had been: a horse could be crippled if it stepped into a wolf's paw print.

CHICKENS AND EGGS

Sailors in the past thought it unlucky to refer to eggs directly while at sea.

When eggs are "set" (placed) under a hen to incubate, there should be an odd number, or else they will not hatch or will all be roosters. They must not be set on a Sunday.

Double-yoked eggs are supposed to be unlucky.

Break the shell of a boiled egg after eating it: that will prevent witches from using it to travel in, over land or water. The same action also protects all sailors at sea.

INSECTS AND SPIDERS

A ladybug is yet another creature that it is bad luck to harm. It can tell an unmarried girl something about her future husband: if she catches one and then releases it, it will fly off in the direction from which her future husband will come.

A bee-sting is not necessarily all bad luck: it is reputed to be able to prevent or cure rheumatism.

A swarm of bees settling on a roof is an omen that the house will burn down.

But if a bee settles on your hand, try not to be frightened: it is a portent that money is coming to you. And if the bee settles on your head, it's even better: it means you will achieve greatness.

Bees must be told all the news about the household of the keeper. The death of the keeper must be announced to them; someone close to the deceased person, such as the child or surviving partner, must rap on each hive three times, saying "The master is dead!" or else the bees will desert you. In the past hives were often draped with black crape as a sign of mourning.

A spider once hid the baby Jesus from the soldiers of Herod by weaving a web over him. That is why spiders are good luck now, and why some say it is unlucky to harm one.

You'll be going on a journey soon if you catch sight of a spider running down its web in the afternoon.

If you shut a spider in a walnut shell that you hang around your neck, you will ward off the plague for as long as it's alive.

A moth flying around your lamp late at night portends the arrival of a postcard. If it makes two circuits of the lamp, there will be a letter; and if three, a parcel.

A moth or butterfly seen in the room of someone just dead is supposed to be the late person's soul. Needless to say, it is bad luck to kill it.

According to some, however, a white moth inside the house or trying to enter it means death.

In some places butterflies have been viewed favorably, as deserving protection. One old superstition regards butterflies as souls, lingering after the deaths of their owners. In some places they have been thought to be the souls of unbaptized children, which cannot enter Heaven.

If the first butterfly you see in the year is white, you will have good luck all year.

A cricket in the house singing its unmistakable song brings good luck to everyone therein.

FISH

A dream of fish means that someone near to you is expecting a child.

Superstitious anglers think it's unlucky to get married at a time when the fish aren't biting.

SLEEP AND DREAMS

If you see a lizard in your dreams, you are being warned that you have a secret enemy.

The way to preserve the fidelity of your husband is to sew a swan's feather into his pillow.

The symbolism of dreams can be perverse. It is said that if you dream of death, it's a sign of a birth: if you dream of birth, it's a sign of death.

Dreams of acorns are portents of pleasant things to come. If a woman dreams of eating acorns, she will gain a comfortable position in the world, with ease and comfort in plenty.

Almonds merely seen in a dream portend a short-lived sorrow. If they are not only seen but enjoyed, the meaning of the dream depends on their taste. If they taste sweet, you'll be lucky; if they taste bitter, then changes that you plan in the near future are risky, and you should put them off for as long as possible.

If a woman dreams that she is nursing a baby, it is a warning that she will be deceived by someone whom she greatly trusts.

Seeing a baby in a dream signifies that you will make new friendships in the near future, perhaps even have a new love affair.

Riding a bicycle in a dream portends bright prospects when you are riding uphill, but can be a warning of imminent misfortune if you are riding downhill.

Dreams of birds in flight are portents of prosperity.

Dreaming of a freshly made bed with snowy white sheets signifies the early end of some worry that has been oppressing you.

A new lover in a woman's life will be foreshadowed by dreams of making a bed.

If candles seen in a dream are burning with a clear and steady flame, you are surrounded by trustworthy friends and kinsfolk, and your prosperity is securely founded.

It is traditionally supposed to be a very bad omen indeed to see a crow in your dreams: it betokens nothing but grief and misfortune.

Dreaming that you are dancing is a good omen. It signifies that good fortune—something unexpected—is on its way to you.

To dream of near ones who are no longer living indicates that something is amiss in your life at the relevant time. If in your dream the dead person speaks to you specifically, what they have to say is of great importance.

Dreaming of diamonds signifies that you will be honored in the near future.

Dreaming about dogs suggests that your friends will be constant and true.

A dragonfly that is perching on some object indicates that you will soon be having guests— who may be hard to get rid of.

If you dream that you are being driven in a vehicle by someone else, you will soon have some luck with money.

Not surprisingly, dreams of well-tended gardens are viewed by the superstitious as representing peace, security and all good things.

Dreaming of strangers' faces indicate that you'll soon be changing your place of residence.

A neglected, overgrown garden represents your neglect of yourself and your own deepest needs.

Dreaming of falling indicates a deep insecurity about one's ability to maintain self-control or control of one's situation.

Gloves in a dream represent troubles with business or the law. However, they are a hopeful sign, indicating that you will arrive at a settlement that benefits you.

TRADES AND PROFESSIONS

SEAFARERS AND FISHERMEN

If you throw back the first fish you catch, you'll be lucky in your fishing for the rest of the day.

A voyage begun on Friday will have bad luck.

Sailors' womenfolk must not attend to their hair after nightfall, for it will bring harm to their loved ones at sea.

CHURCH PEOPLE

It is good luck to encounter nuns—but not if they are walking away from you.

In Cornwall it was believed that you could neutralize the bad luck that followed seeing a minister of the church if you immediately touched some iron.

PERFORMERS

A production will be ill-omened if there is a mirror, or real flowers, onstage.

It is bad luck to say the last line of the play during rehearsals.

Shakespeare's tragedy *Macbeth* is notoriously regarded as unlucky to perform. Actors never mention it by name, calling it simply "the Scottish play."

AROUND THE WORLD

There is a superstition in Iceland that if you don't get at least one piece of new clothing to wear for Christmas, the Christmas Cat will come and get you. It provides the perfect excuse to go shopping.

In the Philippines they say that wearing polka dots on New Year's Eve will attract money and wealth in the future. The polka dots symbolize coins.

Some Koreans believe that if you cut your toenails after dark, the discarded cuttings can form a spirit which can hurt you.

In Korea some drinkers think it's bad luck to order bottles of beer in even numbers. So if two Koreans are drinking, they'll often order three beers.

In Burma children are taught never to awaken anyone too abruptly, in case their wandering soul does not have time to return to the body—in which case, they will die immediately.

GENERAL

If you blow out all the candles on your birthday cake with the first puff you will get your wish.

Children's common terror of stepping on a crack in the sidewalk finds expression in a sinister old rhyme:

"Step on a crack, break your mother's back."

To avoid catching a cold during the winter, you need to ensure you catch a falling leaf on the first day of fall.

The best doctor is the seventh child of a seventh child.

The opal is reputed to be unlucky to all except those born in October. It is particularly bad luck to have an opal engagement ring.

Parents and teachers still sometimes tell their charges that "a blister will rise upon one's tongue that tells a lie."

The Blarney Stone is a stone set in the wall of the tower of Blarney Castle in the Irish village of Blarney. Kissing the stone, while hanging upside down, is supposed to bring the kisser the gift of persuasive eloquence.